To my father Edwin Goodwyn and in loving
memory of Beatrice, my mother

ENGLISH TEACHING AND MEDIA EDUCATION

Open University Press

English, Language, and Education series

General Editor: Anthony Adams
Lecturer in Education, University of Cambridge

SELECTED TITLES IN THE SERIES

The Problem with Poetry
Richard Andrews

Writing Development
Roslyn Arnold

Writing Policy in Action
Eve Bearne and Cath Farrow

Secondary Worlds
Michael Benton

Time for Drama
Roma Burgess and Pamela Gaudry

Thinking Through English
Paddy Creber

Teaching Secondary English
David Curtis

Developing English
Peter Dougill (ed.)

Reading Against Racism
Emrys Evans

Children Talk About Books
Donald Fry

English Teaching and Media Education
Andrew Goodwyn

English at the Core
Peter Griffith

Literary Theory and English Teaching
Peter Griffith

Lesbian and Gay Issues in the English Classroom
Simon Harris

Reading and Response
Mike Hayhoe and Stephen Parker (eds)

Reassessing Language and Literacy
Mike Hayhoe and Stephen Parker (eds)

Assessing English
Brian Johnston

Lipservice: The Story of Talk in Schools
Pat Jones

Language and the English Curriculum
John Keen

Shakespeare in the Classroom
Susan Leach

Oracy Matters
Margaret MacLure, Terry Phillips and
Andrew Wilkinson (eds)

Language Awareness for Teachers
Bill Mittins

Beginning Writing
John Nichols *et al.*

Teaching Literature for Examinations
Robert Protherough

Developing Response to Fiction
Robert Protherough

The Making of English Teachers
Robert Protherough and Judith Atkinson

Young People Reading
Charles Sarland

English Teaching from A–Z
Wayne Sawyer, Anthony Adams and
Ken Watson

Reconstructing 'A' Level English
Patrick Scott

School Writing
Yanina Sheeran and Douglas Barnes

Playing the Language Game
Valerie Shepherd

Reading Narrative as Literature
Andrew Stibbs

Collaboration and Writing
Morag Styles (ed.)

Reading Within and Beyond the Classroom
Dan Taverner

Reading for Real
Barrie Wade (ed.)

The Quality of Writing
Andrew Wilkinson

The Writing of Writing
Andrew Wilkinson (ed.)

Spoken English Illuminated
Andrew Wilkinson, Alan Davies and
Deborah Berrill

ENGLISH TEACHING AND MEDIA EDUCATION

Andrew Goodwyn

Open University Press
Buckingham • Philadelphia

Open University Press
Celtic Court
22 Ballmoor
Buckingham
MK18 1XW

and
1900 Frost Road, Suite 101
Bristol, PA 19007, USA

First Published 1992

A catalogue record of this book is available from
the British Library

Library of Congress Cataloging-in-Publication Data

Goodwyn, Andrew, 1954–
    English teaching and media education / Andrew Goodwyn.
      p. cm. – (English, language, and education)
    Includes bibliographical references (p.) and index.
    ISBN 0–335–09790–1
    1. English language – Study and teaching (Secondary) – Great
Britain. 2. Mass media – Study and teaching (Secondary) – Great
Britain. I. Title. II. Series: English, language, and education
series.
LB1631.G634 1992
428'.0071'273—dc20
                                        92–8563
                                        CIP

Typeset by Graphicraft Typesetters Limited, Hong Kong
Printed in Great Britain by Biddles Limited, Guildford and Kings Lynn

Contents

General editor's introduction

In many other parts of the English speaking world, including the Principality of Wales, 'viewing' is well established as part of the English curriculum alongside reading and writing, speaking and listening. It is a matter of some astonishment, as well as concern, that this is not true of the English curriculum in England. Yet the media, especially television, is the main means of cultural transmission in our society and it is a well attested fact that many students spend more hours in front of a TV screen than they do in a classroom. None the less we have been very reluctant to educate school pupils in how the media operates, even though this task has been placed into the hands of the English teacher by the introduction of the National Curriculum in England and Wales. As Len Masterman has shown in his own books there is a long standing tradition amongst English teachers, traceable back to the work of Matthew Arnold at least, that their task is to defend young minds against the corruption of the mass media. It is salutary to remember what Raymond Williams said as long ago as 1961 in *The Long Revolution* that the masses are always other people, never ourselves.

In his own introduction to the present volume Andrew Goodwyn refers to this uncertainty felt by many English teachers in respect of the role of Media Studies, those who 'suffer particularly from tensions brought about by valuing and enjoying the media whilst deeply distrusting it'. This tension, or schizophrenia, has never been far away from the minds of English teachers who are still prone to wish to protect others from what they themselves enjoy in private. (Worst of all perhaps are those who take the opposed view: those English teachers who proudly boast that they do not even so much as possess a television set.)

It seems to me self-evident that no teachers of English in the 1990s can afford not to watch television nor can they afford not to read the tabloid press. We cannot engage with the minds of young people whilst cutting ourselves off from the culture that sustains many of them.

In arguing for a central role for Media Studies within the English curriculum

Goodwyn adopts a particular stance. There are many who would claim that Media Studies is a subject in its own right which should not be contracted into the narrow confines which it inhabits as a part of a wider English programme of studies, 'ghettoized' in Buckingham's words quoted in this book. None the less Goodwyn's argument is a potent one and, indeed, if Media Studies does not appear within English it is likely that it will continue to be unregarded given the pressure of the increasingly wide-ranging curriculum in most schools. What has been encouraging has been the way in recent years in which Media Studies at GCSE and A Level have become a growth industry: they are no longer seen as the preserve of the less able or the illiterate who study films and video instead of books.

Although he has his reservations about the metaphor Goodwyn quotes a well-known passage from the Kingman Inquiry into the Teaching of the English Language: 'Round the city of Caxton, the electronic suburbs are rising. To the language of books is added the language of television and radio ... the processed codes of the computer. As the shapes of literacy multiply, so our dependence upon language increases' and he claims that here, as in the subsequent Report of the Cox Working Group on the National Curriculum in England and Wales, is 'the first official endorsement of media education within English ... neither very radical nor entirely coherent'.

None the less it is there and we can only be surprised that it has taken so long for this endorsement to appear when Media Studies have been so long established elsewhere. In his review of the history of media education Goodwyn goes some way towards showing the reasons for this and the hostility that English teachers have often had towards the media in general – 'discriminate and resist' became the slogan. Resistance, thankfully, being no longer possible, the English teacher needs to embrace the opportunities that media education provides; given the insights of post-structuralist criticism we have now come to extend our awareness of the wide range of 'texts' that we have available to us in our classrooms and in the experience of our students.

Andrew Goodwyn's present volume provides practical help for the teacher wishing to include media education within the work of the English classroom. It is a balanced and considered account which avoids the extremes which characterized much of the emerging climate of Media Studies in the 1960s. By its very nature the field itself is difficult to define and can sprawl until it becomes all encompassing. Goodwyn charts a smooth passage through this difficult territory which should prove of help to all English teachers intent upon introducing this area of work into their curriculum.

Anthony Adams

Preface

There has never been a more important time for all teachers to come to terms with the power, influence and educational potential of the media. The decade of the 1990s is unquestionably the time for English teachers to find a consistent approach to media education, making it a part of their normal classroom work. The emergence of media education as a part of English has been a slow and painful process; but the National Curriculum, with a legislative stroke, has made media education chiefly the responsibility of English teachers. Now the English-teaching profession and teachers generally have to decide how to implement this National Curriculum edict.

All teachers, but most crucially English teachers, seem to fall into three groups with quite different attitudes towards media education. For some teachers media education is still alien territory and the impetus to understand it may come entirely from the legal momentum of The National Curriculum, 'We have to teach media education so how do we do it?' For others, teaching about the media has always been a part of their work and The National Curriculum has simply provided a useful validation, but one which does not yet go far enough. This second group may also already be teaching Media Studies at GCSE and A Level.

There are a great many other teachers, I suspect, who are somewhere in between the two groups. They feel that young people, future citizens, must understand and recognize not only the importance of the media but must come to some understanding of how it works. This latter group suffer particularly from tensions brought about by valuing and enjoying the media whilst deeply distrusting it. For example, they find aspects of television, especially documentary and drama, of real significance but fear what seems to be the narcotic and mindless appeal of soap operas, quiz shows and the like. They read *The Guardian* or *The Independent* and catch occasional glimpses of *The Sun* or *Mirror* expressing a combination of horror and amusement that such writing can exist. When pupils talk about their parents' reading of the tabloid press they feel uncertain how to react but they are always impressed by the way pupils seem able to mimic the papers' style with such accuracy and panache.

This book is aimed at all of these groups and others who are interested in trying to decide where we place media education in school. I am quite certain that the great majority of media education belongs within the English curriculum but there is plenty of disagreement and debate about such a view (see Chapter 1). English, I believe, with its primary attention to reading, responding and evaluating the text and to the individual's response in relation to that of others', is the best place for media education in school. This definite siting of media education is not in contrast to the idea that media education should be a cross-curricular concern for all teachers. Nor is it in conflict with the rapid development of a more specialist area called Media Study. The latter is a vital extension of the work that begins in English and then becomes a specialist study in its own right. This book does not in any way set out an alternative to Media Studies and in that sense is not aimed at teachers who see themselves exclusively as Media Study specialists. Equally this is not a sociological text and I hope that the reader finds the relatively occasional use of specialist terminology to be appropriate and helpful, never overwhelming. Where then does media education fit into the specialism of English?

A good secondary school will have in the future, a clear policy on media education across the curriculum, paying proper attention to continuity with the work already carried out in Key Stages 1 and 2. It will have an English Department which places great emphasis on media education in Key Stage 3 combining analytical and practical work. That department will devote a good deal of its attention to the media in Key Stage 4 and, whilst also running a Media Studies course for the most interested pupils, will continue to demand a sophisticated level of knowledge about the media from all its pupils. In this way all pupils can continue their development as active readers of the media through formal study and through being citizens in a media-soaked environment.

In order to invite the three groups considered above into this discussion about media education as well as interested teachers from other disciplines I feel the need to provide not just a convincing argument about our current needs but also a rationale that helps to relate past opinions and prejudices to contemporary issues. The first two chapters will attempt to outline the foundations for my approach, making an analysis of the long debate about the relationship of media education to English. Chapter 1 reviews the remarkably rapid coming together of English and media education during the 1980s and the role of the National Curriculum in this process. Chapter 2 then goes much farther back and outlines the way English and Media Study evolved during the earlier part of the century and their generally antagonistic and hostile relationship. It is only through a consideration of this difficult evolution that certain forces and influences that are currently still powerful can be recognized and understood. It was not until after a number of major shifts in English and in Media Study that it become possible for the two subject areas to move towards each other. Having covered a necessary historical background in the first two chapters, the third and fourth look closely at definitions of the media and the challenges of media theory itself.

The subsequent four chapters are related specifically to the ways in which media education can grow out of traditionally accepted English practices and complement and develop them. In Chapter 5 I shall examine the relationship between the attention English teachers give to the four language modes and ways of extending and improving pupils' learning in the modes through media-related work. Chapter 6 takes some key media areas that English teachers tend to find difficult, examines them in depth and offers ways of working that should both overcome difficulties and integrate such media work with existing good practice. Chapter 7 has an entirely practical focus and provides a series of examples of topics and schemes of work that demonstrate the rich possibilities brought to English through media education. The final chapter brings together the various arguments rehearsed in the book and looks towards future developments. It analyses the potential of new technologies and tries to map out an English curriculum that, in addition to literary and linguistic education, has media education at its heart.

As a part of the continuing discussions in the book I refer to The National Curriculum where relevant. I do not begin from the premise that The National Curriculum and its particular powers are the source for the development of media education within English. This legal positioning is not a cause but an effect of a gradual and, in my thinking, inevitable change in English, and in all school teaching. However, the nature of the National Curriculum means that its status and momentum will have a range of effects and I consider these throughout the text.

I hope that this book will be of use to all teachers of English, whatever stage of their careers they have reached and whatever level of responsibility they have assumed. Equally I hope the ideas and suggestions in the book will be of help to student teachers and new entrants to the profession who may still be surprised by the nature and degree of resistance that they find to media education. Media education, like Language in the National Curriculum, is not an area of learning about which one can be merely neutral, it is too important for that. Understanding and appreciating how the media works and how we both enjoy and struggle with its texts leads to radical questioning about how all texts are produced, controlled and disseminated or withheld. Just as we all believe that pupils should leave school having achieved a high level of print literacy, so it is time to ensure that citizens of the twenty-first century are equally literate in reading the media.

Acknowledgements

I should foremost like to thank my wife Janet Goodwyn for her constant help, encouragement and for undertaking so readily such demanding editorial duties. I should also like to mention my children, Tom and Helena, for making it all seem worth it.

I should like to thank the various members, staff and students, of the Department of Arts and Humanities in Education and of the Secondary PGCE course at Reading University with whom I have worked over the last few years for their daily help and their good fellowship and most of all my former partner in English, Ron Middleton.

I should like to thank the Series Editor, Tony Adams, for his enthusiasm for my ideas and for his kind support and encouragement throughout the writing of the book and the publisher John Skelton, for his tolerance and patience.

1 The relationship between English and media education

English as a school subject is changing. There are a number of reasons for the change but one of the most important originates in a broadening of the subject to include media education. The change is in process and so there is a considerable degree of uncertainty about what English is going to look like in the future. The formal inclusion of media education within English, effectively from 1989, through the documents of The National Curriculum (*English 5–16*), is one cause of the uncertainty. What had been a rather haphazard and erratic development as more English departments began to include media-related work in their normal practice was suddenly a uniform and consistent requirement. However, as the emphasis on media education within English was part of an already existing momentum, the National Curriculum has simply provided a recognition, albeit a rather vague one, of the progress already made towards a proper integration of the two subjects. The vague and rather scattered references to media education in English in the various National Curriculum documents will not in themselves resolve uncertainties. English teachers should not compound their uncertainties by looking to add on bits of media work, they need instead to rethink and reformulate aspects of English itself.

Defining the relationship

At times one has to state the obvious in order to question it and this is especially true within a subject like English, a subject with which everyone has some kind of familiarity. English, almost everyone agrees, *is* a subject, and a very important one, although it is rare to find any total agreement on what it is. It is much easier to define Media Studies although some might dispute whether it is a subject at all. My starting point is a broad definition of English as the study of the production and reception of texts in English and the contexts in which those processes take place. A text is broadly defined as any meaningful utterance and so includes speech and media output as well as writing. Contexts include everything from society and culture to two speakers in conversation.

This broad definition places media education firmly within the domain of English but a great deal more elaboration is needed to explain my case. Proponents of media education and Media Studies have reacted negatively to the official positioning of media education within English (Masterman 1985, Buckingham 1990a,b). It is worth examining the official rhetoric and some reactions to it in order to provide some understanding of the current demands being made upon all English teachers. The origin of those demands will be examined in more depth in Chapter 2.

English and media education or Media Studies?

My own view is that English and media education are already integrated up to GCSE/Key Stage 4 and remain closely aligned during the examination years. I consider that the majority of media education is, and should be seen as, a part of English. I have given a broad definition of English above but Cox and his committee offered what they saw as five principal approaches to teaching English (DES 1989: 2.20–2.27). Their explanation of differing positions within English is a very valuable one and points out that what we call a subject is in itself highly problematic. Any subject contains oppositions and dialogues and, whatever committees may say, will continue to do so. The Cox Committee rightly recognized the range of viewpoints within English but did not attempt to prescribe any one.

Media Studies as an academic subject has a fascinating background of its own. Like English, it has been the site of numerous battles between champions representing differing views of the subject. The way its various underlying theories have evolved is well documented (there is an especially useful overview in *Culture, Society and the Media*, Gurevitch *et al.* 1982). Media Studies in school has often been defined (see, for example, Buckingham 1990a) as if it is far more homogeneous than English and, although I think that this is accurate, it does not mean that we can assume that in itself it is fixed.

English has a relatively brief history as a subject (see Eagleton 1983, Doyle 1989, Goodson and Medway 1990) and the nature of its origins are much debated, although there is a rough agreement that it began to appear in the late nineteenth century. The study of the media (Masterman 1985, Alvarado *et al.* 1987, Inglis 1990) is certainly more recent in origin but the novelty of the two disciplines is very similar. Over the last 15 years the two 'subjects' have been coming much closer. The narrowing of the gap stems from their common concern with textual understanding, analysis and production. In school the subjects begin to divide into separate specialisms once the students have become, almost exclusively, critics.

In order to establish a sense of the present continuites in English and media education it is important to start with the primary curriculum and move up the Key Stages. Until 1989 'English' did not exist in primary schools. The great majority of work associated with activities called English in secondary and tertiary education was called in primary schools 'Language'. This definition stems from the holistic nature of the primary teacher's role. When particular attention was being paid to the production (speaking, writing) or receiving (listening, reading) of language then 'Language work' was the most helpful term. This helps to explain the evolution of the BFI/DES document *Primary Media Education: A Curriculum Statement* (Bazalgette 1989). The document argues first for media *education* rather than the narrow, more specialist sounding term media *study*, and it is significant that the Cox Committee (DES 1989: 9.6) selected this terminology. The use of the term *education* is a key point in showing the commonality of English and media education. They are both principally concerned with the broad area of language and, in particular, with the reading, production and interpretation of texts. The BFI/DES document throughout refers to media *texts*.

If we take these questions:

- *Who* is communicating, and why?
- *What* type of text is it?
- *How* is it produced?
- *How* do we know what it means?
- *Who* receives it, and what sense do they make of it?
- How does it *present* its subject?

they might just as readily be applied to a poem, a play or any other literary work as to media text. The fact that these are given as the significant questions to raise with children about their understanding of media texts (Bazalgette 1989: 8) suggests to me how clearly media education comes under the Language brief in Key Stages 1 and 2. Cary Bazalgette goes even further than this in her chapter in *Reading, Learning and Media Education* (Potter 1990: 22) where she argues that ' "Literacy" needs rethinking.' She concludes by highlighting the way the questions above provide a framework for extending primary teachers' conception of literacy: 'I would argue that the questions this structure makes possible are the ones we need in order to extend the possible meanings of any text, and to extend the range of texts available to us. This means, extending our pleasures as well as our understandings' (Potter 1990: 25). In the primary years it seems that Language, i.e. English and media education, not only spring from the same source but are part of a definite, particular curriculum area.

In English or across the curriculum?

In the secondary curriculum there has been a considerable debate about whether the study of the media should come principally from within a single

subject or should be cross-curricular. Bazalgette and others, most influen-
tially Masterman in *Teaching the Media* (1985), argue for media education
to be seen as cross-curricular. In the primary school this works very easily
for the same reasons as Language, the teacher's holistic role. Masterman
argues that media work should be handled chiefly in this way in the secondary school and is very hostile to the traditions of English teaching as he de-
fines them. He argues that English teachers have viewed the various forms
of the media 'as threats to language and literature through their debasement
of cultural standards' (Masterman 1985: 254) and that such teachers ignore
the institutions and contexts in which all texts are produced. Although he also
acknowledges that younger English teachers may make a more 'honourable'
contribution to media education he wants to spread media education across
the curriculum to ensure that it escapes from being presented in a narrow,
prescriptive manner. The BFI document *Secondary Media Education: A
Curriculum Statement* (Bowker 1991), includes a whole chapter on Media
education through the curriculum (pp. 68–86) but its attitude to English
teachers is quite different to Masterman's. The BFI book points out how all
subjects can contribute to pupils' media education and that '. . . it is important that secondary schools do not leave full responsibility for media education to the English Department' (Bowker 1991: 3), a view with which all
English teachers can agree.

Media education across the curriculum is an admirable goal but potentially a misleading one. There is absolutely no contradiction between media
education operating in every school subject whilst also receiving specialist
attention in English. Every teacher should help pupils with their language
development and the Language Across the Curriculum (LAC) movement
highlights how crucial it is to make attention to language the brief of every
teacher but also the specialist responsibility of a few. Many teachers,
especially some English teachers, think of the LAC movement as having
failed when in fact its success is evident everywhere. Their disappointment
stems from the impossible expectations raised by some missionaries for the
movement. Supporters of media education might learn from what happened
to LAC. The latter's considerable success lies in the fact that it influenced
the language awareness of all teachers and also reinforced the key role of the
specialist contribution of English (DES 1975). In *Watching Media Learning*
Buckingham is concerned that 'media education will simply be "ghettoized"
within English. The fact that media education has been so successful in gain-
ing a place within English could easily be used as an argument to prevent
it permeating elsewhere – and even from continuing to exist as a separate
subject' (Buckingham 1990b: 10). A different, more positive, approach,
however, is what is needed. Media education is essentially placed within
secondary English, and its influence and significance across the curriculum
can be extended from that base. This remains as an essential issue for
teacher education, both initial and in-service.

English and media texts

My case for media education in English is a simple one and has been partly introduced through my comments above on the idea of 'texts'. The best formulation of how we conceptualize the media is the same as it is for more traditional print forms, through text. We experience written texts of all kinds and then we begin to differentiate between them and to appreciate inter-textuality. As we begin to produce texts the same applies, we gradually become familiar with and adopt different ways of writing them. We experience media texts ranging from newspaper and magazine print to television and radio programmes and begin to recognize a great deal about them and then to 'read' them more precisely. Our production of such texts tends to be mainly through talk and writing but the tape recorder and the video camera provide approximations of the 'real thing'. Student's written texts have the same relationship to published books as do their media texts to, for example, broadcast programmes. We are all exploring the reception and production of texts.

English teachers develop a number of essential elements in human understanding. One is personal response, the area designated by so many media specialists as a kind of impossibility (see Gurevitch *et al.* 1982) but by so many English teachers as their *raison d'être* (for example, Protherough 1983). For media specialists the personal has been seen as a form of disengagement, a retreat into a spurious individuality for what scope has the individual in a society utterly controlled by an establishment? However, English teachers have premised almost all of their work in literature and language on the assumption that each pupil can construct and refine a personal meaning.

A great deal of the debate in this area seems to me to be misdirected. Many recent examinations of reader response theory (for example, Corcoran and Evans 1987, Hayhoe and Parker 1990) have shown how the personal is inextricably bound up with our impersonal response, i.e. all those elements, social, cultural, ideological and so on that make up the context within which we can respond. The personal response invokes the second area, our interpretative response. At the same moment as the personal response all the above factors are creating possible readings. The individual's particular perspective is potentially present when we read any kind of text, media or other and is struggling with a host of possible interpretations. English is concerned with recognizing the nature of response, enjoying it and sharing it with others. The teacher of English has a key role in developing the interchange and enrichment of the personal and the impersonal. Whether reading a media or print text we are working out its meaning, sometimes with great concentration and at other times in a far more relaxed way. We can increase and refine our response through discussion, imitation, analysis, writing and so on.

A third key area is discrimination. The term has been much reviled by media theorists, especially Masterman, as part of a redundant liberal humanist methodology mixed up with highly suspect values; the ghost of Leavis is seen to be stalking popular culture (see Chapter 2). There are two powerful reasons why notions of discrimination and value have to be accepted as part of media education as well as English. The first is that all teachers and children clearly operate within value systems. Media theorists tend to attack dominating value-laden ideologies but without accepting that their influence provides many of the meanings that media texts actually make. Should media theorists dictate that teachers must be above engaging in discussions of why some programmes matter so much to some people? Children, whenever they are allowed to exercise a choice, are discriminating. They are making judgements, considering comparisons, laughing or crying. Teachers certainly take care when selecting which texts they want their pupils to engage with. At its worst Media Studies has evolved a sterile and reductionist approach (Buckingham 1990a,b) whilst having pretensions to offer its students a chance to escape to some theoretically value-free haven. Students do learn about both the importance and limiting effect of values and media education/English is probably the most vital subject in this respect. All texts are replete with values and textual study allows students to gain some detachment from, but also deeper understanding and enjoyment of, values that they can analyse for themselves.

Some of the most lucid analysis of the rigidity and narrowness of aspects of what might be called traditional media study come from *Watching Media Learning*, 'While there remain those who regard media education as a kind of crusade to save the working class from ideological manipulation, there are many teachers who are seeking to develop a more productive approach' (Buckingham 1990b: 10). He points out that for students in supposedly open media teaching in fact 'there is often little space for them to generate their own readings, or to explore the contradictory pleasures which such texts offer. It is as if potentially subversive or dangerous meanings must be policed out of existence by rigorous, rational analysis' (p. 8). I would not claim that all English teachers are willing to explore all subversive readings and I agree that their literary training sometimes gets in their way. However, I would emphasize that English is the forum in which considerations of meaning and value are under constant review. Children explore these notions through language and reflect on and study that language as a part of their English work.

The chapter 'Teaching the Text: English and Media Studies' in *Watching Media Learning* further supports the idea that good practice in English and media education are developing along similar lines. In that chapter Andy Freeman argues that 'the distinction between English and Media Studies may be much less clear-cut in practice than it would appear to be in theory' (Buckingham 1990b: 197) and that developing models of reading of texts are eroding any substantial subject differences even between GCSE Media Studies and GCSE English Literature (pp. 210–11).

One place where this erosion is especially striking is in the wider reading element of Literature syllabuses. Students there are encouraged to choose their own texts and to develop their own approach. In my own department pupils were invited to include media texts in their studies and in my in-service work I have found this to be an increasingly common approach amongst English departments. As I noted earlier it is at the point where the division into specialist subjects occurs that students are expected to become critics. The introduction of GCSE Literature has in fact changed the approach to texts which had characterized O Level Literature. Apart from a few syllabuses like the Cambridge Plain Texts all pupils taking O Level Literature had to respond to their texts in a uniformly narrow way, basically the critically appreciative essay. Now a wide range of approaches, still including the above, is encouraged and, to an extent, required.

Buckingham in defining existing differences between the Media Studies and English characterizes these literary approaches, new and old, and all aspects of English as 'practices' whereas Media Study is defined in terms of 'concepts' (Buckingham 1990a: 10). Media study 'concepts' include media institutions, representation, media language and forms and conventions. English practices in the broadest sense include reading, writing, speaking and listening. These broad practices are then subdivided: writing, for example might be expressive, imaginative, expository and so on. Buckingham's distinction is perfectly accurate and certainly does illustrate the historical differences in the evolution of English and of Media Studies. However, I hope I have shown that these differences are not really a part of current practice in the first three Key Stages where media education operates chiefly within English whilst retaining a cross-curricular dimension. The differences are still present in GCSE syllabuses though not necessarily in the clasroom. I hope that my argument shows how logical it is that media education should continue to develop as part of English during the last two years of compulsory education.

At present we have three GCSEs. The largest in terms of pupil numbers is English, which contains language, literature and media work. Then comes English literature which still contains all these elements but with far more attention, despite wider reading, to traditional literary genres. Finally there is Media Studies, distinguished by its attention to concepts rather than practices or named texts or even types of text. One of our great problems with the latter is a real lack of empirical knowledge about whether pupils/ students can learn these concepts. Questions concerning what is developmental about media concepts and whether there are stages related to pupil's age or intellectual development at which these concepts should be introduced remain largely unanswered. In English the situation is quite different; there has been a great deal of research in to what helps pupils to learn about reading, writing, speaking and listening. I am not arguing for any intrinsic superiority for English as a subject, but pointing out that there is a far more established body of research in the subject. This research includes extensive studies of concepts investigated in relation to children's learning. A concept like 'story' is a prime example (e.g. Applebee 1978, Protherough 1983). This body of knowledge in English, coming from a developing pedagogy linked to the real experiences of pupils and teachers, should be the basis for the gradual construction of our understanding of how children conceptualize the media.

However, one major existing weakness in English is that its emphasis on practices mean that both its students and its teachers seem to ignore concepts at present. I very much agree with David Buckingham when he comments that English teachers even treat publishing as 'a general cultural activity or indeed as a kind of charitable service for distressed authors' (1990b: 22). There is some real truth in this criticism and I think GCSE Literature should demand that its students investigate the institutions that both support and control reading and writing. English teachers do a great deal of work related to institutions, for example, about censorship, and they do explore the backgrounds of some authors, the social and cultural contexts of some key texts and so on, but none of this in a systematic manner.

One striking point about this gap in English is that it parallels the pedagogic difficulties in Media Study. How do you teach about media institutions in any meaningful way? Again, do we know whether the concept of institutions can be explored usefully at any particular age or stage of development? If there is a really significant difference between the specialisms at this level of study then I am not sure that we are clear about it yet. It does seem that the specialism is as much to do with the attention paid to the textual content of the subject area, i.e. to devoting time to reading either media texts or literary texts rather than any more profound distinction. I am not arguing for the demotion of Media Study at GCSE level/Key Stage 4 or above. It is students and teachers who wish to specialize and to follow their interests in depth. I do think, however, that English, as the broadest subject area, and English Literature as the principal area for textual study, should increase their attention to media texts (see Chapters 6 and 8). There is a strong argument for Dual Certification between Media Study and both English GCSEs although there is no expectation of this happening in the near future.

English and media education are working in partnership already in many primary and secondary schools. The existing divisions between English and Media Study at GCSE level are very real but are as much to do with the historical and abstractly theoretical origins of the latter. Media education just like Language education must be maintained across the curriculum but English and media education in their focus on texts, contexts and the response of readers form together a powerful, dynamic specialist subject.

HMI and Kingman, leading up to The National Curriculum

The Cox Committee paid reasonably close attention to media education within English but initially it is worth placing this attention within the context of comparative neglect found in other official publications of the 1980s. In the HMI document *English 5–16* (DES 1984) there are some tiny beginnings that are worth noting. The objectives for 11 year olds include 'Follow the plot of a story or a broadcast play written for this age group' (p. 6), 16 year olds should be able to 'Read newspapers, magazines and advertising material critically so as to distinguish between unbiassed information and attempts to manipulate the reader; and apply similar critical attitudes to television reporting and advertising'. In stressing that pupils should 'have some ability to judge the value and quality of what they read', the HMI extended this point to include media texts, insisting that pupils should 'Have some ability to apply similar judgements to entertainment in other media – theatre, cinema or video films, television and radio' (p. 11). When considering language the HMI added, almost as an afterthought, that 16 year olds should 'Recognise that language is a spectrum which ranges from simple factual statements to complex uses of the sound and texture of words, of rhythm, of imagery and of symbol; and that such effects are not confined to poetry but occur in daily life (e.g. in advertising)' (p. 12).

What is most striking about this embryronic national curriculum is its tension, it is caught between an attempt to fix English into a series of quite pedagogically conservative statements whilst recognizing that such statements immediately exclude much else. There are many statements in the document that, retrospectively, might seem very open, for example, the injunction to 'Recognise and distinguish between explicit and implicit meanings in what they read' (p. 11). This kind of approach is exactly what brings media education so positively together with English. However, the few actual references to media areas in the HMI document seem to me to come chiefly from the discriminate and resist tradition (see Chapter 2). The HMI wanted English teachers to help their pupils sort out fact from opinion, especially when its source was something as dangerously entertaining as advertising but they did not expect such work to start until the pupils were relatively sophisticated. The whole document shows a kind of grudging acknowledgement about the media whilst ignoring the areas that really matter to most children, and their parents, fiction and narrative. There is no suggested media related work for 7 year olds and only one idea, see above, for 11 year olds.

In the follow-up document *English 5–16: The Responses to Curriculum Matters 1* (DES 1986) a single paragraph no. 44 (p. 18) is devoted to Media Education:

> Groups with special interests in media education expressed a general welcome for what was said about the various media (film, television and video, audio, and non-book print), but suggested that it did not go far enough. They called for closer engagement with the social significance of the media and of language in general and urged the case both for media education to its own right and for a more full and circumspect use of the media in English and in other subjects. Like 'knowledge about language', media studies require wider debate and are

likely to call for substantial in-service training. The aims and objectives of media education need to be arrived at in respect of all the subjects of the curriculum. If an agreed curriculum on these matters is not arrived at, diverse and hidden ones will inexorably emerge.

Apart from being remarkably vague, especially the last, rather extraordinary claim, the paragraph seems to suggest that the HMI saw media education as still stemming from special interest groups. Their final point in *Conclusions* reinforces this, 'Those who raised the topic of media education emphasised the pervasiveness of the media in all our lives and the subtlety of the ways they shape attitudes and opinions; their case for more explicit attention in schools to the media and to key ways in which they influence and impinge upon our lives is strong but not confined to English (DES 1986: 19).

Overall these two documents are important for their slight but clear indication of the importance of media education in English. Their tone is very cautious and conservative and in relation to media education the style is somewhat simplistic, but, for HMI documents, such comments may still be considered highly significant. The documents are most illuminating for the revealing contrast that they provide with the Cox Committee. The HMI already had their eyes on other matters, namely their particular baby, knowledge about language, still too young to be rendered in upper case or as an acronym. This obsession led directly to the production of The Kingman Report (DES 1988).

The Kingman Report did not have as its specific brief any aspect of media education and so references are scattered and tend to be merely illustrative examples. This led the committee to miss many opportunities to show the relevance of knowledge about language to pupils and teachers alike because the media are one of our richest contemporary sources of language in use. As Professor Widdowson indicated in his *Note of Reservation* (DES 1988) the whole report is flawed by refusing to consider what English is actually for.

The Cox committee, partly through acts of definition, made very clear the need for explicit attention to media education in English. In contrast, in Kingman 4.13 (DES 1988: 37) there is an indicative section about writing:

> In making their own newspapers, radio broadcasts or television news bulletins, they [pupils] will need to discuss explicitly a whole range of language issues. These are not confined to syntax and lexis; pupils, will soon realise that a news story has a different impact according to the order in which the facts (or even the pictures) are arranged. Word processors are useful here.

Two things here are remarkable: 'pupils will soon realise' – this begs so many questions! – and '(or even the pictures)', which reveals an entirely superficial degree of attention to how newspapers communicate meaning. There is another comment in similar style in 4.29 (p. 42):

The language of newspapers, for example, and indeed of television and radio, merit attention in the classroom. Comparison of newspaper headlines and the recognition and clarification of ambiguity, or drawing parallels in, say *The Sun*, *The Independent* and *The Times* makes pupils realise that language can obscure truth as well as reveal it.

This style is rather like the grudging tones of the HMI documents, 'merits attention' being an especially good example. The Kingman Report only advanced the cause of media education in English in this haphazard and rather indirect way. The Cox Report signals an altogether different approach.

English, media education and the National Curriculum

One of the few genuine links between Kingman and Cox is the heading placed at the top of Section 9 of *English 5–16* (DES 1989), 'Round the city of Caxton, the electronic suburbs are rising. To the language of books is added the language of television and radio . . . the processed codes of the computer. As the shapes of literacy multiply, so our dependence upon language increases.' (DES 1988: 2.7; quoted in DES 1989: Section 9). I feel that the city/suburb metaphor is completely inept but presume that the Cox Committee wished to show some continuity with their predecessors. It is, however, far more important to look on Cox as a decisive break with this earlier tradition of grudging acceptance of the inescapability of media influence.

My intention here is to avoid a simplistic reiteration of the pronouncements of the committee (DES 1989: Section 9) and to interpret what was actually meant. The Cox Report is the first official endorsement of media education within English and it is neither very radical nor entirely coherent but it does reflect the changes going on in schools in the 1980s that Kingman and the HMI seem chiefly to have ignored.

One of the most welcome elements in Section 9 is the clear stress on media education in relation to 'Children's practical understanding of how meanings are created' (Section 9.2). The whole section combines Information Technology (IT) with media education to focus on this idea of making meanings 'Media Education and Information Technology alike enlarge pupils' critical understanding of how messages are generated, conveyed and interpreted in different media' (Section 9.1). This is a central point but not very clear in its expression. Is the implication that computers and televisions have screens and so they are really rather similar? In that sense we know they are not. The whole section is rather bland, lumping IT with media education as though that were sufficient to prove likeness, e.g. 'Many aspects of media education and IT involve the use of machines: still cameras, video computer terminals etc.' (Section 9.5). If this were enough of a rationale then we might include cookers and fridges and therefore Home Economics. The greatest weakness of the section is that it fails to do full justice to the significance of either IT or media education and only touches on the potential for interrelation.

However, in other ways, the section is a triumph, especially in the manner in which it shifts the whole emphasis of media education in English away from a reluctant, resistant mode towards a positive and developmental challenge for pupils and teachers alike. It stresses 'critical understanding' (Section 9.2) which is an open rather than closed definition. It celebrates practical work (Section 9.2) and stresses the active involvement of pupils (Sections 9.5, 9.6 and 9.8). It takes as its key point of reference Cary Bazalgette's definition of media education in *Primary Media Education: A Curriculum Statement* (Bazalgette 1989: 3) and this is well worth quoting in full. The definition in the companion secondary document is almost exactly the same (Bowker 1991):

> Media education ... seeks to increase children's critical understanding of the media – namely, television, film, radio, photography, popular music, printed materials, and computer software. How they work, how they produce meaning, how they are organised and how audiences make sense of them, and the issues that media education addresses. [It] aims to develop systematically children's critical and creative powers through analysis and production of media artefacts. This also deepens their understanding of the pleasure and enjoyment provided by the media. Media education aims to create more active and critical media users who will demand, and could contribute to, a greater range and diversity of media products.

This definition is the informing spirit of the section although the Non-statutory Guidance and the Programmes of Study are not as imbued with that spirit as they should be. The references to media education in the Statutory Orders of the English National Curriculum for Key Stage 3 are helpfully picked out in *The English Curriculum: Media 1 Years 7–9* (Grahame 1991: 22–3).

Another key point to stress is the all-embracing nature of the definition of the content of media education, not only as expressed above but as set out in Section 9.7 of *English 5–16* (DES 1989) 'all public forms of communication including printed materials (books as well as newspapers)'. This is very significant because it asks English teachers to bring that erstwhile sacred object, the book, into the ordinary world of artefacts that have been through a process of production and distribution. Perhaps the statement only hints at this but the opportunity to explore the publishing industry and to problematize the appearance of books in the school and public domains is undeniably present.

A more ambiguous point comes in Section 9.8:

> We have considered media education largely as part of the exploration of contemporary culture, alongside more traditional literary texts. And we emphasise elsewhere that the concepts of text and genre should be broadly interpreted in English. Television and film form substantial parts of pupil's experience out of

school and teachers need to take account of this. Pupils should have the opportunity to apply their critical faculties to these major parts of contemporary
culture.

This paragraph is useful in that it insists that teachers should interpret the
idea of texts and genres in a broad way. However, the purpose of this
broadening is then somewhat circumscribed by the privileging of film and
television. The language of 'apply their critical faculties' has the sound of a
practical criticism exercise based on some notion of good taste.

The media sub-section comes to a close (DES 1989: 9.9) with a far more
valuable and powerful statement about media education dealing with 'fundamental aspects of language, interpretation and meaning' and having 'developed in a very explicit way concepts which are of general importance in
English'. This final acknowledgement that English has a great deal to gain
and learn from media education as it had developed in the 1980s is the ultimate measure of how much progress was made from the HMI documents
of 1984 and 1986 to The National Curriculum of the 1990s. In a sense media
education had finally arrived on the curriculum after a few very uncertain
years and, in my view, in the right place for it to develop and flourish.

2 The story so far

The story of English and Media Education

This particular story cannot begin with once upon a time. As long as there has been teaching of a subject called English, at whatever level, the teachers of that subject have been paying attention, perhaps in the beginning, unconsciously, to what we would now define as the media. English came into being as a subject within higher education and it had two main aims, one to study the literature of the English and second to develop an understanding of the national culture (for useful summaries of the early aims of English see Widdowson 1982: 17–31, Eagleton 1983: 17–54, Goodson and Medway 1990: 47–86). The main practice of English was the reading of Literature and students were to be introduced to texts considered to be of established and enduring value. As far as we know it was certainly not the intention of those who taught this version of English to introduce their students to popular culture, if anything, their mission was to create a profound distaste for all such ephemeral and vulgar productions. However, even then there was an acknowledgement that students might prefer to read other texts than those selected by the academy, some of which might indeed be 'popular'. English has always then had a tension implicit in its structure about what serious readers should read and what they actually choose to read. A similar tension continues to exist in the relationship between present versions of English and media education. Intelligent people are not supposed to indulge in the frothy entertainments of the media yet they certainly seem to do just that. Far more seriously these tensions also raise profound questions about who produces, who controls and who consumes texts?

I am arguing that English, as a field of study, contains by its nature, and always has and will, tensions and contradictions about what its object is and should be (Goodson and Medway 1990). Other subjects, once scrutinized, all reveal the problematic nature of such definitional activity, and the efforts of the various working groups of The National Curriculum Council from 1988 onwards have highlighted this. However, English has definitional difficulties to a unique extent because its very name is ambiguous. The study of English seems to imply many things including a language, a literature and a culture that both contains and is defined by the other two elements. I shall need to return to more current definitions of English, especially in relation to Media Studies, later in the chapter.

English has constantly questioned and reinvented itself and shows every sign of continuing to do so. For participants in the process, whether fully conscious of their involvement or not, the issue might be defined as basically a boundary-drawing exercise, how inclusive is English? I am arguing that the boundaries of English have always included serious attention to the media even though the formal map makers may have hoped to keep media texts outside the conventional territory of the subject.

Discriminate and resist

Although the story does not have a neat, definitive beginning it nevertheless has some critical episodes. The most important of these is marked by the publication in 1933 of *Culture and Environment* by F.R. Leavis and Denys Thompson. The impact of this book and its significance have been well documented (Masterman 1985: 38–70, Inglis 1990: 31–43) and with good reason. The book marks the beginning of the phase in English teaching which might be called the period of explicit resistance to anything to do with the mass media; for a few teachers there is still no conclusive ending to that period. Certainly The National Curriculum documents in English, for all their actual references to media education, remain riddled with contradictions, particularly for the conspicuous absences of key areas of media experience such as serial narratives; these absences can still be traced to the powerful call of Leavis and Thompson 'to discriminate and resist' (Leavis and Thompson 1933: 5).

So much of importance has stemmed from the work of Leavis and Thompson that it requires close attention to appreciate both how English and media education have moved steadily together but also why it has taken so long for them to become a complementary force. Leavis and Thompson intended their book primarily to be used as a textbook in school but also hoped it would be helpful to university students, student teachers and those involved in adult education, debating societies and study circles. It is worth giving this remarkable list to indicate the breadth of their intention and the importance they attached to their message. The message begins in the first paragraph of the book and, I suspect, sounds as if it might have come from one of a number of present-day sources (1933: 1):

Many teachers of English who have become interested in the possibilities of training taste and sensibility must have been troubled by accompanying doubts.

What effect can such training have against the multitudinous counter-influences – films, newspapers, advertising – indeed, the whole world outside the classroom? Yet the very conditions that make literary education look so desperate are those which make it more important then ever before; for in a world of this kind – and a world that changes so rapidly – it is on literary tradition that the office of maintaining continuity must rest.

One of the authors' chief concerns is for what has been lost from society, they have an intense nostalgia for an old order now destroyed by the machine. What concerns us more is the particular roles they cast for the English teacher pitted against the forces of the mass-produced society. These forces were most dangerous for the young (Leavis and Thompson 1933: 3–5):

Those who in school are offered (perhaps) the beginnings of education in taste are exposed, out of school, to the competing exploitation of the cheapest emotional responses; films, newspapers, publicity in all its forms, commercially catered fiction – all offer satisfaction at the lowest level, and inculcate the choosing of the most immediate pleasures, got with the least effort . . . The moral for the educator is to be more ambitious: the training of literary taste must be supplemented by something more . . . We cannot, as we might in a healthy state of culture, leave the citizen to be formed unconsciously by his environment; if anything like a worthy idea of a satisfactory living is to be saved, he must be trained to discriminate and resist.

This polemical and missionary message set the tone for decades to come: discriminate and resist. The English teacher's role was to save pupils from the overwhelming forces and influences around them by training them to resist and thus to defeat them. The defeat was mainly to be achieved by helping pupils to value the great tradition of English Literature (see other works by Leavis).

In many ways this is an evangelical version of the mass media theory of the Marxist Frankfurt school (Gurevitch et al. 1982: Chapter 2). These early attempts to theorize about the media posit the feeble individual overwhelmed by vast and often sinister forces. Later views still recognize the institutional and economic force of the media but restore a sense of the power retained by both the individual and by groups of readers and viewers (see Chapter 3).

The English teacher was handed a torch by Leavis and his followers, a torch which both symbolized individual resistance but also cast a sharp, illuminating light. The simple fact was that you could not resist something without knowing what it was, Leavis and Thompson were committed to 'more consciousness' (1933: 5) about, amongst other things, the media. Culture and Environment is full of examples of media texts which pupils are invited to analyse and, through a raised consciousness, reject. An important, perhaps surprising point is that there is a real and living continuity between the ideas of Culture and Environment and present-day practice in the English classroom. Most current English teachers feel involved in helping their pupils to discriminate and resist a whole range of potential influences whatever aspect of English they are teaching. I think they would claim that their definitions of what they are resisting and how they are discriminating have changed considerably. For example, are there any English teachers who do not wish their pupils to discriminate between texts that explore racist issues and those that are merely racist? The endeavour is surely to help pupils resist insidious racism? The moral fervour and sense of mission are still at the heart of such an approach within the English classroom.

Masterman (1985: Chapter 3) argues very powerfully for a reappraisal of Leavis and even more so for a recognition of the work of Thompson. Masterman's key point is that serious attention to the media begins within the secondary curriculum from this point on and that Leavis and Thompson were advocating such work entirely against the grain of the existing literary establishment. Leavis and Thompson wished all pupils to retain their individuality in spite of 'the possible relation between the standardisation of commodities and the standardisation of people' (1933: 32). They feared that ordinary people would be overwhelmed by the power and influence of the mass media. Their solution was to try to equip all pupils with a kind of mental shield made from the finest literature before each individual went out alone to face these massed media forces.

What Masterman criticizes about their enterprise is that it lacked any political edge. 'In staking out a ground for literary culture as the supreme repository of moral and spiritual values, above and beyond politics, Leavisism was bringing to completion an extended project within "English" which was to be its most crippling legacy to media education' (Masterman 1985: 46). I find this a very clear and reasoned analysis and one that helps us to understand what became known as 'inoculation theory', i.e. that the job of the teacher was to expose pupils to a few media germs so that they would develop a complete resistance to all infection as adults.

The followers of Leavis, notably David Holbrook and Fred Inglis, in his early work do seem to have taken those key terms, discriminate and resist, and to have replaced them with dismiss and reject. Holbrook's *English for Maturity* (1961) contains some prime examples of the virulent hatred of all aspects of the media that this injunction seemed to generate. In a passage concerned with the dissatisfactions that he claims pupils feel with modern life (p. 17), he argues:

> Of such dissatisfaction rock 'n' roll, 'teenage' hooliganism and motor-suicide, are ... expressive enough. What is missing from the music of our young people, from their entertainment, and from their social life together is the germ of positive vitality. They have no cultural sources of succour, to develop positive attitudes to life, and develop human sympathy. The home is afflicted by the influence of the mass media, by the pressure of advertising and by the new illiteracy.

In a more extended passage Holbrook equates the media with all the negative aspects of commercial and industrial society and insists that English teachers in particular must resist all such influences (pp. 37–8):

> We must never give way: we are teachers of responsiveness to the word, in an age when it is possible for even quite intelligent people to believe that a concern for words, for language is 'out of date'. The new illiteracy of the cinema, television, comic strip, film strip and popular picture paper they accept as the dawn of a new era. Many schools are even buying comic-strip books of classics, and many see films and television as the means to new forms of teaching, whereby a deep impression can be given of some aspect of the world with the minimum use of words . . . we are weary of dealing with pupils from an environment which has given up reading and in which the word is so badly damaged by popular media there is a great appeal in the 'visual theory' – that words no longer matter to a world with television: or that the way to literature is through illustrated strip-books.

Holbrook's argument is now a very familiar one, he simply equates everything produced by the modern media technologies with a kind of illiteracy, by his definition no media text can be serious or even genuinely meaningful. His work is typical of that very powerful element of English teaching mentioned above, the discriminate and resist faction, yet his views are even more hostile. The tensions in the writing are very evident, 'even quite intelligent people' take the media seriously, that 'quite' says so much. Homes are 'afflicted' by the media, the word is 'badly damaged', the language insists that there must be a vast and sinister plot by media producers to corrupt and destroy every aspect of what Holbrook might call decent civilized life. It seems as though English teachers in particular must fight a desperate rearguard action otherwise Literature will not survive. Holbrook's rhetoric is highly typical of one, prominent viewpoint.

Even now some English teaching still can be dominated by a blank rejection of what pupils, and their parents, choose to read and view. This attitude at its worst creates a total disjunction between pupils' experiences of reading an extensive range of texts and the expectations they are confronted with by teachers whose self-appointed mission is simply to supplant their pupils' readings with 'real' literature. This over-simplified yet extreme version of the message of *Culture and Environment* shows exactly how a lack of political and also economic awareness may make some English teachers mislead their pupils into thinking that there are two types of cultural object: the best, a small proportion of textual production which is somehow above and beyond the forces of ordinary cultural conditions, and the rest, which belongs in a vast, bazaar-like cultural basement.

To return to Leavis and Thompson, what unites them with present-day English teaching is that in their work they wished to take into account the full range of experience that pupils or students brought to their reading and reflecting. Therefore they took the productions of the media absolutely seriously and treated them as representative of the whole culture. Retro-spectively it seems fair to say that their literary sensitivities led them to take the proliferation of text-based productions, particularly newspaper and maga-zine advertisements, far too seriously. What they ignored were the institu-tional frameworks that were then emerging in which the media texts were produced. It is this fatal omission which Masterman rightly selects as the crippling legacy to media education.

The grammar-school English teaching of the early post-war years was dominated by the Leavisite approach both to literature and to popular culture as manifested in the press and advertising: 'We must introduce our pupils to suitable classics; firstly because they offer contemporary society what it needs so badly – an objective set of values; secondly because we can never be sure that boys [sic] discover even the most obvious ones for themselves. Our classics offer some protection against the assaults of Ad-vertisement, Propaganda, and "Pulp Literature"' (*The Teaching of English*, Association of Assistant Masters in Secondary Schools 1952: 32). This text also devotes a section to newspapers and suggests beginning exercises involv-ing rigorous content analysis (pp. 83–4). The struggle between proper and serious attention to aspects of the media and a fierce safeguarding of literary 'standards' was prevalent throughout the decade. The work of some of Leavis's followers went much further than Leavis himself and Holbrook's work represents one of the most vitriolic and apocalyptic views of the media but it also signals the beginning of the end, in the late 1950s and early 1960s, of the dominance of such opinions.

Personal growth

The 1960s, despite the pronouncements of Holbrook and others, saw some radical changes in English teaching. Whilst these changes were not directly concerned with media education they were indirectly of great significance for a definition of English with an inclusive view of media texts. A text like *Growth Through English* (Dixon 1975) exemplifies the radical nature of the changes. Dixon's book results from the Dartmouth Seminar where lead-ing figures in English teaching from the UK and the USA met to discuss common concerns and interests.

The book mainly explores the model of teaching explicit in its title: that pupils in English would steadily grow as individuals through their explor-ations in language and literature. The content of English was principally there to foster this growth. Allusions to the media are few and slight, most references are to pupils watching and discussing films or television without any comment about the media-related nature of these activities. In a sense this shows that such activities were seen as normal and unproblematic but it also reveals that their function was simply to extend the process of personal growth. Watching was something you did in order to talk about the subject or content of the programme and your own views and feelings. Only one comment harks back to the discriminate and resist tradition. Where Dixon discusses the need for an English department to have structure and consistency in a world where new kinds of change, for example, rapid population movement, are affecting society, he says: 'Popular culture, depending so strongly on the media for mass-communication, is subject to continual change and some debilitation perhaps' (1975: 83).

The comment is not at all Leavisite, least of all in tone, but it suggests an uneasiness with the constant flow and energy of the media. I think one can detect here a strong wish for the comparative stabilities of literature (see Dixon 1975: 83–92). The personal growth model is extremely flexible and inclusive as a basis for an English curriculum but in relation to media texts *Growth Through English* seems relatively rigid and narrow.

Peter Medway, in his chapter 'English and English Society at a Time of Change' (Goodson and Medway 1990), comments specifically (pp. 32–3) on the heavy emphasis placed on the personal growth model in the late 1960s by writers like Dixon:

> English no longer, as in 1958, helps the student to identify his or her 'real self' in conformity to institutional values. It does not prepare children for approved roles ... An explicit claim of English is to help students with a central predicament of modern youth, that of making their own order and learning to cope with the 'inner cultural discord' induced by a pluralist society ... What is to be recognised as the 'real self' is decisively the private self.

The personal growth model, Medway argues, constantly privileges not only the subjective response but also the domain of feeling over the domain of analysis. It is at this time that the previously well-established tradition of formal grammar teaching was decisively challenged, officially by Bullock, and, to a large extent pushed aside (see Keith in Carter 1991: 69–103). Grammar teaching was certainly the domain of analysis and personal growth and parsing had little in common. In all the welter of change and debate the role of the media was given little new attention within the English classroom except in the way outlined above: as it played a part in most pupil's individual experience so it was of value, particularly for discussion (see Dixon 1975). But if, in a sense, media education was growing – albeit slowly – within English the attitudes of educationalists generally towards the mass media largely remained in the resist category. Masterman gives a clear outlines of these views (Masterman 1985, Chapter 3: 43) citing *The Crowther Report* (DES 1959) as a striking example of the official anti-media rhetoric: 'There is also in our view a duty on those who are charged with the responsibility for education to see that teenagers, who are at the most vulnerable and suggestible stage of their lives, are not suddenly exposed to the full force of the "mass media" without some counter-balancing assistance.' This notion of counter-balancing seems to fit exactly with the emphasis of the term resist.

Thompson had a further chance to put forward his views as the editor of *Discrimination and Popular Culture*, a collection of essays published in 1964 as a direct result of the NUT conference on 'Popular Culture and Personal Responsibility' (see Masterman 1985: 43) held in 1960. This collection posited a slightly more useful role for the media but still argued principally, as the title suggests, for an evaluative and highly selective approach, the teacher's job being chiefly one of arbiter of particular media texts and not as concerned with the media in any institutional or contextual sense.

English in the 1970s continued to develop and expand the personal growth model until the work of Britton, Barnes, Rosen and others shifted attention more specifically to the role of language in the whole school environment. Their pioneering work in Britton's *Language and Learning* (1970) and *Language, The Learner and the School* first published in 1969 (Barnes *et al.* 1986) moved attention to the dynamic role of language in all learning and to the need for schools to take every aspect of language seriously. This work led directly to the Bullock Report and to the Language Across the Curriculum Movement which dominated the latter part of the 1970s and the early 1980s. As a part of this movement it is possible to see media education continuing to develop its place within English. Britton (1970: 264) comments:

> Once we recognise the value of books as a source of experience, we must admit as similar sources the visual – verbal media of film, television and stage-play. I think it is a matter of time (and money for equipment) before this realization affects the school curriculum: out of school, at home, the equivalence is already apparent.

Whilst not centrally concerned with the media in his work Britton nevertheless acknowledges both their potential and the fact that their importance was yet to be fully felt. The difference in attitude between such a comment and that of Thompson, Leavis or Holbrook indicates the beginning of a great change.

The preachers of culture?

There are two significant texts in the early 1970s that help to chart the developing role of the media within English teaching but also indicate the continued and associated tensions for the teachers. The first, and most important, is *Mass Media and the Secondary School* (Murdock and Phelps 1973), the results of a Schools Council sponsored research project. To my knowledge this remains the most thorough piece of research about media education in this country and it is still fascinating to read. The research documents many significant points about schools, teachers and pupils in relation to the 'Mass-media' and provides us with a very valuable body of evidence about attitudes to the media in the early 1970s. I shall be highly selective in picking a few points of special significance for *my* present concerns.

A point concerning the 'diffuseness of the English teacher's role' (Murdock and Phelps 1973: 14) made by the researchers remains as vital now as it was then. In surveying the attitudes of various teachers to 'aspects of their job' English teachers placed Subject Instruction first, Moral Education second and then Education in Human Relationships third. Science teachers were the same in the first two categories but placed Education in Human Relationships fifth. From this evidence and associated questions the researchers note (p. 14):

> ... at the very centre of his [sic] definition of his job as a specialist in English, the English teacher is faced with a considerable degree of uncertainty. While, on the one hand, the training that most English teachers receive encourages them to define themselves as specialists in that corpus of literature which is widely held to be the principal repository of the 'cultural tradition', in the school situation they are often expected also to assume the responsibility for educating pupils in human relationships, which inevitably means some attempt to handle the mass media. Many English teachers are thus pulled in two direction simultaneously, and must inevitably make some attempt to come to terms with the situation. Basically they have two options. Either they can define their job quite narrowly as teaching basic linguistic skills and handing on the 'literacy tradition', or else they can see themselves more broadly as specialists in social communications including the mass media.

The researchers argue that some English teachers were taking the second option and broadening English but that a considerable number were tending to erect a barrier between the classroom and the world outside and to fall back on a definition of their job which stresses the transmission of literary values (p. 14).

However, English teachers, whether positive or hostile about the media, were definitely in the forefront of awareness about pupil's engagement with the media. Seventy per cent of English teachers recognized that the media had a 'Great or moderate amount of influence on their pupils' work' (Murdock and Phelps 1973: 21), almost every other subject was below 50 per cent. English had the highest percentage of teachers who noticed the presence of media catch phrases in pupils' language and their pupils' increasing interest in pop music and fashion (p. 18). At the same time only 2 per cent of English teachers thought that the media increase pupils' scientific knowledge compared to 39 per cent of Science teachers. English teachers felt the presence of the media most acutely in their pupils' imaginative written work though only 17 per cent of them saw this as a fundamentally bad influence (pp. 24–5). My interpretation of these various findings is to suggest that English teachers are clearly shown to be starting to grapple with the media in their everyday work but also shown are the limitations of their view of what the media provide for pupils and adults. The 2 per cent figure perhaps reveals how little English teachers actually knew about some areas of the media such as television.

The section of the report 'Teachers in the classroom: using mass media material' (pp. 32–52) provides some of the most intriguing information about English teachers. Teachers overall are divided into four categories (pp. 33–42):

- Approach one, mainly favourable towards or untroubled by the media but almost never bringing it into the classroom.
- Approach two, deeply against media influence and so excluding it deliberately from the classroom.
- Approach three, very hostile to media influence and so introducing it into the classroom to develop pupils' discrimination and resistance.
- Approach four, viewing media as an enriching part of experience and so dealing with it in order to increase both this enrichment and pupil understanding.

The writers trace the origins of Approaches two and three to the work of Arnold, and in particular, *Culture and Anarchy* (1869), Leavis and Thompson, *Culture and Environment* (1933) and Frank Whitehead, in *Directions in the Teaching of English* (Thompson 1969). All of these figures are from the field of English, and so the implication is that the main proponents of English Literature as a subject are the main opponents of the mass media and its supposed negative influences. This part of the study is not broken down into figures by subject teacher although there are some revealing comments quoted from various English teachers. For Approach four, the authors cite the influence of Richard Hoggart's *The Uses of Literacy* (1957) and the early work of Marland (Thompson 1969, Marland 1977). Both these writers are also from the English field but champion the resilience of the individual and the richness of the media.

What we gain here is a helpful picture of the growing awareness of the need for English teachers to think through and find a position in relation to media education. English teachers in the study fall into Approaches two, three and four, all concerned with and about the media, their attitudes covering the entire spectrum from positive to negative. This finding is backed up by the frequency with which English teachers were using mass media material – 'Several times a term or more' – in the classroom. It is worth quoting the table of results in full (Table 1).

English teachers were evidently making considerable use of the media in their work and their reasons are especially interesting: for example, 23 per cent stated that their media work provided a starting point for subject work, 36 per cent insisted that it was to help pupils defend themselves against the media and 35 per cent to encourage discrimination and appreciation.

This invaluable study provides us with concrete evidence of the mixed views and feelings of English teachers about the aims of media education but it shows equally that the majority of English teachers considered it a part of their job to enable pupils to engage with media texts. Already Approach four

Table 1   Frequency with which teachers used mass media material (the figures represent percentages of teachers in English and in Science)

Media	Several times a term or more		Never	
	English	Science	English	Science
Newspapers	67	47	4	29
Television	67	47	8	28
Magazines	41	27	19	36
Radio	27	11	39	64
Cinema	32	6	23	69
Pop records	25	5	35	80
Comics	9	1	58	88

was followed by a substantial minority of English teachers. Before making a final comment on the study, however, it is worth turning to a second key text of the 1970s, *The Preachers of Culture* (Mathieson 1975).

Mathieson makes several points about the mass media in relation to English teaching and about the report itself. One of her main points echoes that of Murdock and Phelps that English teachers are caught between varying tensions within the subject and educational change generally. Her position is relatively conservative and ultimately she recommends a more formal and literary kind of English as the only means by which the various tensions developing in the subject might be resolved. *One* of her key reasons for suggesting that attention to the mass media in lessons is not appropriate in English is expressed as follows (1975: 219):

> Unless the school becomes a part of the mass media, it is difficult to see how these lessons will appear to the children as anything more than pathetic imitations . . . The whole approach demands plentiful time, reliable and easily available equipment, carefully planned links between lessons and, above all, delicacy in the treatment of emotionally cherished material. After deciding what his aims are in this area, the teacher needs to be far less of an amateur than he generally is, to do anything in detail about the complex organisation of press, advertisements, television programmes and promotion of pop records.

Her argument actually suggests that the English teacher needs to take media education more seriously and adopt a systematic approach when teaching. This argument remains valid and will continue to do so. What we find then in this book and that of Murdock and Phelps is that the period of blanket rejection of the mass media is almost over. Both books highlight the tensions for many English teachers in attempting to work within a literary heritage model and a form of cultural analysis. In the background to their work is the coming of the comprehensive school forcing all English teachers to review the content of the English curriculum. The two books capture both a time of change and the inevitable anxieties that accompany it. They help to clarify why from the mid-1970s onwards, although the debate continued, the nature of the argument began to change.

Bullock and after – from preachers to agnostics

The Bullock Report itself, although it devoted Chapter 22 to 'Technological Aids and Broadcasting', did not make any radical or challenging comments about media education, rather it reinforced the steadily growing idea that consistent and serious attention should be paid to media texts: 'Television is now part of our culture and therefore a legitimate study for schools' (C and R 295). The Report argues for more systematic attention to television in particular (DES 1975: 22.14):

> One of the most powerful sources of vivid experience is the general output of programmes on television, particularly documentaries and drama. Many teachers are already basing a good deal of classroom work on such programmes. In secondary schools ... teachers brought the experience of the television screen into the classroom, preparing for evening programmes and following them up the next day. Some classes were reading the texts of television plays with enjoyment and others were writing scenes for themselves. In a few schools we came across the serious study of the medium of television itself ... We believe that in relation to English there is a case for the view that school should use it not as an aid but as a disseminator of experience. In this spirit we recommend the extension of this work. Although there is unquestioned value in developing a critical approach to television, as to listening and reading, we would place the emphasis on extending and deepening the pupil's appreciation.

In Appendix six of Marland's *Language Across the Curriculum* (1977: 300–301) we have one of the clearest indications that media education had become part of the normal work of the English classroom. Marland goes further than the Bullock Committee when commenting on the Report (p. 300):

> I hope that once and for all its recommendations have pulled television out of 'audio-visual aids' and placed it in a position analogous to books ... it should be in the continuum of talk, reading and literature, for the approach to television is analogous to the approach to literature.
>
> The emphasis should not be on criticism – that is, the 'Reading and Discrimination' approach. It should certainly not be heavily influenced by concentration on what is judged to be meretricious in an attempt to drive that enjoyment out of pupils' lives. The sharing of enthusiasm is more educative than the attempt to persuade to see the faults in certain programmes.

Marland also discusses the fact that much of the above work will be 'especially the province of English' (p. 301) but that there will be a need for a specialist option in the 4th and 5th year.

Another striking development of the 1970s was the use of film in English, see, for example, *Film in English Teaching* (Knight 1972). The most notable feature of this work was the development of Film studies as an O Level and also as a part of sixth-form work. Many English teachers were pioneers in introducing their pupils to the serious study of film. However this attention to film, i.e. a serious, artistic body of work, in fact illustrates the continuing tension for the English teacher in resisting popular culture and in discriminating for pupils by selecting significant films for them to study and appreciate.

A final important influence at this time came from linguistics, notably the work of Halliday and the 'Language in Use' team. The influence of linguistics is acknowledged and evident in the work of Britton, Barnes, Rosen and so on, cited earlier. However, from the late 1960s onwards, linguistics has had a direct influence on English teaching and this can be seen in specific projects or movements, e.g. 'Language in Use', 'Language Across the Curriculum', 'The National Writing Project', 'The National Oracy Project' and 'Language in the National Curriculum'. The various official reports published during the period, including most notably those produced by HMI (see Chapter 1) make it clear how this linguistic influence is becoming prevalent. The Kingman Report marks, so far, the high point of that influence. Ronald Carter, Director of the LINC project, remarked at a talk (given at Nottingham University, January 1992) that he was initially astonished by the bibliography of the Kingman Report because it seemed so entirely to relate to his field, Linguistics, and to relate so little to the body of research about language developed within English teaching.

The importance of the influence of Linguistics for the development of media education in English is far reaching. Linguistics calls for the systematic study of language and does not begin by giving privilege to certain kinds of text. Even more importantly Halliday's work is concerned with language as a meaning making system and so all texts can be approached as significant. Potentially this places the study of an advertisement alongside that of a poem or the study of a speech from Shakespeare alongside that of a present-day politician. Such an approach is one of the informing spirits of the LINC project in the early 1990s. On the basis of a linguistic approach the systematic study of texts is almost certainly going to include the whole range of media texts and to accord them real status as powerful and meaningful.

It seems reasonable to suggest, on the basis of this evidence from the 1960s and 1970s that English teaching was consistently and quietly absorbing what we now call media education. Most of this work centred on the press, television and film and anxieties about quality were prevalent. These anxieties remain in the official documents of the 1980s such as HMI reports

and the Kingman Report (see Chapter 1) but much less so in the actual practice of English departments. This gradual absorption of media work into
English contrasts dramatically with the extraordinary rigidity of approach
prevalent in media study theory as epitomized in the work of the BFI and of
Screen in particular in the 1970s and early 1980s. In this sense English was
moving and redefining itself to absorb media education whilst media study,
ironically, was creating its own version of discriminate and resist.

3 The media context

Defining 'the media'

Views about what the media are and how they can be defined have changed over the years and continue to do so. However, it is still much easier to find a relative consensus about what is meant by 'the media' than it is to find a consensus about 'English'. The media are usually defined as a list, in, for example, the BFI document *Secondary Media Education: A Curriculum Statement*, the media include 'television, film, video, radio, photography, popular music, printed materials, books, comics, magazines and the press, and computer software' (Bowker 1991). However as Masterman asks in *Teaching the Media* '. . . how is it possible to make any conceptual sense of a field which covers such a wide range and diversity of forms, practices and products?' (1985: 19). His answer, and that of others, has been to stop worrying about a narrow and prescriptive definition of the content of the media and, instead, to look for unifying principles in the study of the media; in other words to delineate a theory that would help to generate understandings about the media and in this way arrive at a definition of 'what' they are (see Chapter 4). Underlying this approach is another, fundamental, principle that definition of the media will not start from any heirarchical value judgements. The way in which we attempt to comprehend the media should not be premised on a concept of discrimination.

Before returning to a content definition in relation to English I should like to clarify this point about value. I have stressed in Chapter 1 that pupils and teachers are necessarily engaged in dialogue about what they do and do not value. Inevitably all judgements, all explanations, must be affected by the cultures and ideologies of each individual and of the dominating communities around the individual. It is not a contradiction to suggest that part of the struggle with such forces and their attempts to insist on *one meaning* is the necessity to resist, to play with and to explore meanings. The English teacher can be far more aware than pupils can of the limitations imposed by cultural influences and to this extent and no more, that teacher should refuse to start from the narrow and prescriptive perspective of value. There must always be tension in this position and it is possible to see this tension as highly productive.

The teacher can start from the position of selecting exactly what the class is to work on: this would be typical at the beginning of most schemes of work in English. The teacher might have chosen newspapers as the focus for a class of any age or ability. Such a choice is clearly either relatively value free or extremely value laden depending on whether that teacher's ultimate question is either what are newspapers and how do they work, or, why are the newspapers that I, the authority, read, better than most others? Research shows that teachers tend to read exclusively the broadsheet newspapers (see for example Murdock and Phelps 1973: 3–5). No teacher can avoid the latter question internally but it can, and should, be avoided whilst children are forging their own answers to the first and far more important question.

Relevant areas of the media: some initial distinctions

It is very important to explore initially what the English teacher might define as the appropriate areas of the media to include in English. I have suggested (see Chapter 1) that media education belongs chiefly in English but that there is no contradiction between such an approach and the fostering of media education in every other subject and as a consciously highlighted cross-curricular concern. Every teacher using English as a medium is a teacher of English. Every teacher using the media either directly or indirectly should also be a media teacher. Such teaching can cover a whole spectrum of concerns from working with concepts to illustrating a subject-specific point, for example, painterly allusions in advertising and their relation to understanding the history of Art.

To some extent then every teacher can deal with some or all of the list: television, film, video, radio, photography, popular music, printed materials, books, comics, magazines and the press, and computer software. However the English teacher, and the school (see Chapter 8), can define the media in relation to the needs of pupils so that coherence and consistency is brought to pupils' experiences in and out of school. The areas where there is most obvious overlap in school terms are popular music with Music, photography with Art and now Design and Technology and computer software with Information Technology/Computer Studies.

In the case of Music there is one possible, rather simplistic but effective distinction that might be made. The Music department might concentrate on the music and the musical context which includes the powerful institutions that influence what music is produced. The English department can focus on the means by which that music is packaged and advertised and mediated through the press, magazines, etc. This is simplistic as a distinction because the music industry embodies all these elements. However, the importance of popular music to pupils is so great that the combined efforts of the two departments can only be productive in helping pupils towards more understanding as well as enjoyment of the music they like whilst recognizing that the pleasure is still constructed and mediated and, at times, controlled and exploited by socio-economic forces.

There has been a great deal of work using photography in a media education context both in primary and secondary schools (Bethell 1984, Bazalgette 1989, Goodwyn 1990, Bowker 1991) and such work seems to have stemmed partly from English teachers' interests in autobiography, narrative and documentary. There is no reason why such work should suddenly disappear from English to another curriculum area and this provides an exact example of where the school and its departments are unquestionably the best judges of appropriateness. Photography provides the potential for many kinds of work from the particular study and analysis of genres or individual photographers to the development of practical skills in pupils. This is still an emergent and evolving area and, as such, an open and dynamic one. It seems essential that a medium such as photography should be approached in many subjects but that the chief responsibility for structuring pupils' understanding should be jointly organized by the English and Art departments in the secondary school.

Computer Studies has not, historically, taken a media education role in relation to software; its principal aims have been to develop technical understanding and programming competence. Information Technology (IT), which is not a substitute subject but a different concept in relation to computers, has a less clearly defined position at present as an area for the development of pupils' critical awareness. It is rapidly developing in schools in a multitude of forms (POST 1991). However, as there are many problems obstructing its potential to change the nature of learning in schools, it is still hard to predict what its long-term effects will be.

At present the National Curriculum Documents in English tend to stress the importance of word processing as the English teacher's chief concern. It is clear that all pupils must have the entitlement to produce writing using a word processor and so reach the stage of competence through which they can understand what happens to the writing process when they can manipulate text electronically (see, for example, IT'S English (NATE Computer Working Party 1989)). We have yet to develop a full understanding of what happens when a group of pupils compose together around a screen but research so far suggests that the language environment may be particularly rich for all involved. This latter, collaborative activity involves many elements of learning AND the most fundamental is the reading of the screen. Reading a screen has many aspects of the conventional page but there are enough differences to suggest that the learning moves into the sphere of media education.

The screen contains a text, possibly several texts which have a relationship to the system, e.g. particular word processing software, which produces the text. The system provides both power and constraint and pupils bring to the system differing degrees of knowledge, allowing them more or less power over the system. The system itself has been produced by an institution, possibly commercial, possibly educational, probably both. Pupils can learn to use the system, to compare it with other systems and they should come to a critical understanding of what these systems mean in themselves as part of the socio-economic structure of their culture. In what part of the curriculum will pupils develop this fuller understanding of what the power of information technology actually means?

First, it is evident that such understandings may only be fully realized in a specialist context such as Media Studies or Information Technology at Key Stage 4. Second, in order to provide for this understanding the process needs to get off the ground as soon as possible and to be consciously addressed by a whole school policy. Third, the English Department has a vital part to play in taking an active not a technically passive role. Pupils, in developing their competence in say, word processing, should also be developing their critical understanding of what word processing means. In this way then English should approach IT in the context of media education and not simply by operating a writing competence model.

Relevant areas of the media: some definitions

Most missionaries for media education begin with an account of the awesome influence of the media, their comprehensive penetration into our everyday lives and the various statistics that we have as evidence of just how many hours teenagers, especially American teenagers, watch television (see Masterman 1980, 1985, Lusted and Drummond 1985). I take it that we can accept much of this as evidence whilst reserving some very real questions about what influence means in relation to the media (see Chapter 4). What we need to consider here is what content from the list is relevant and in what ways? Now that I have made some tentative suggestions about the differing contributions that school departments might make I need to make a case for how the media should be defined in relation to children's learning in English. The following sections are intended both to clarify and raise some key points, and the practical examples in Chapters 5–7 are intended to provide both an extension of these initial points and a more detailed supporting argument.

Television

We must start with television because it can claim the most universal presence of any of the media. For children in particular it is a far more insistent medium in that watching is likely to come well before reading. By the time pupils enter secondary school they are likely to have watched many thousands of hours of television. What can English teachers do with this extraordinary flow of potential meanings?

I would argue that the first thing they should do with this medium and all the others in the list is to problematize it. As an analogy and starting point it is worth asking what English teachers do about the meanings that their pupils have made from their reading? English teachers usually want to know something about pupils' reading because they need to assess pupils' competence and because it is of personal and professional interest. In order to provide continuity secondary teachers need to identify what pupils have gained from their primary, school-based reading and from their reading at home. If basic questions about books are broadened to include the reading of all texts, e.g. what are your favourite texts, how much do you read, do you read on your own, what do you know about texts and who produces them? These questions immediately begin to unsettle simplistic notions about who has 'read' the most and why. Suddenly it is likely that all the pupils have read thousands of texts, some pupils predominantly in print, other pupils predominantly in audiovisual form. In both cases English teachers fully expect to change and improve their pupils' readings of texts in as rapid and effective a manner as possible. Some texts will be read and discussed as a class, others may be read privately but might be recorded in a diary, some texts may be studied very extensively over a period of weeks and so on.

As Bazalgette argues 'The arguments against bringing print literacy and audio-visual literacy closer together are based on the simple empirical observation that everyone can watch TV but not everyone can read a book' (Potter 1990: 19). People feel that reading is a high-order skill that has to be taught but that watching is somehow natural and easy. Bazalgette points out that:

> . . . if children were 'bathed' in reading to the extent that they are bathed in TV watching – and I don't think even the most relentlessly literary household could ever equal the numbers of hours children spend, with friends, siblings and parents, learning how TV is watched – then who is to say that most children wouldn't come to school with basic reading skills already acquired and we would be saying that children 'naturally' learn to read in the home environment?
>
> (Potter 1990: 20)

We certainly do know that pupils are interpreting television and creating meanings quite at odds with those intended by programme makers. We all have to learn to read television texts and in so doing become more critical, more appreciative and potentially more selective.

If English teachers are balancing the importance of printed texts with others then all pupils can contribute their expertise and enthusiasms for what they enjoy. Just as pupils produce very different readings of the books they encounter so they will of other texts; one of the most exciting and developmental areas of the English classroom is this flow of possible meanings and interpretations. At present some English teachers would feel saddened when they learn that a pupils' home contains no books but they would feel quite differently if the home contained no television. The lack of television would be taken to signify something much more dignified and important and certainly not economically determined. I consider this a paradox and I feel that all teachers, but especially English teachers, should recognize the potential contradiction in their views about watching as opposed to reading.

Understanding of the media seems best expressed as a spiral of development with constant returns to the same content but bringing each time increased critical awareness and sharpened perception (Bazalgette 1989, Bowker 1991). Using this approach it becomes far less important to worry about which aspects of television are most suitable for, say Year 7, and much more vital to begin to build a sense of how to establish and build on understandings. In this way a class might identify from its own research which is the favourite/most watched programme by that class or even the whole of Year 7, perhaps offering tentative reasons at that stage as to why it is such a 'successful' programme and why it appears when it does in the schedules. The class might then move to apply and try to answer the key textual questions:

● Who is communicating and why?
● What type of text is it?
● How is it produced?
● How do we know what it means?
● Who receives it and what sense do they make of it?
● How does it present its subject?

These questions provide a systematic approach whether the text is the current Saturday morning programme for children or a documentary.

English teachers constantly make use of televised books for a whole host of reasons, frequently because they recognize that the television text may make a different kind of impact to the printed one. I would argue very strongly that the teacher who sees the television text merely as a substitute for the printed one, whatever the ability of the pupils, is misleading that group. The relationship between the texts is of crucial significance to all readers. Pupils and teachers may well have strong views about which is a better text but such judgements are almost meaningless without some understanding of the medium through which the meaning is produced.

I shall return to the topic of television in a number of ways but I should like to raise one other point at this stage about how we can move on from the arguments concerning the supposed effects of watching television to those focused on what television represents to its audiences. The worries of all teachers about the potentially harmful effect of television are well documented, one particularly interesting result being the DES 1985 publication *Popular TV and Schoolchildren: The Report of a Group of Teachers* (most readily available in Lusted and Drummond 1985). The report contains a range of views and so presents a very mixed argument about what to do about television. But, as David Lusted very precisely observes, the report's importance lies in the fact that it moves the argument on from effects to representation: 'That shift from a set of worries about television's effects to a set of questions about television's representations of the social world is central and crucial. It must be held to as a direction for the future of schooling about television' (1985: 11). What is predicated here is the need for the English teacher to investigate television along with the pupils, to get at and consider what is being represented and how. This investigation must include therefore much more than the classic serial. It must encourage pupils to reflect on soap operas, comic programmes, cartoons, quiz shows, chat shows and so on. In certain respects documentary and other 'serious' forms are much less interesting because their intention is principally to inform. What a current soap opera about urban life may represent may be far more challenging and demanding for pupils and teachers to investigate.

Film

Of all the media film is the one least likely to arouse concern as a form. It comes with all the necessary status to take its place alongside traditionally canonized books as part of art rather than commerce. In the 1960s and 1970s film was the respectable end of the media spectrum. Cheap and reasonably reliable equipment meant that schools could use film in a range of ways for study, entertainment and so on. The result was a rapid growth in Film study as such and its rapid validation by examination boards. English teachers seem to have liked film because of its artistic seriousness which in turn meant that it was worth studying; pupils also liked this rather out of the ordinary treat so different from most of their lessons in school.

The introduction of cheap and reliable video equipment (see below) has meant that film is just as much used in school as it was in the 1970s but its special status has largely disappeared. The movement of the 1980s has been for all, and especially English teachers, to broaden their approach to the media generally and so film has taken its place within that context and certainly no longer dominates. During the early 1980s film also lost its status amongst children and adolescents, many cinemas underwent changes of use and only in the later 1980s was there a real revival in watching the big screen.

The BFI concentrated many of its early educational efforts at providing materials for use in schools which would give some critical insights into the film industry and also to the language of film (see the Resources list). This material appears to have had little effect nationally, local pockets of enthusiasts certainly made considerable use of these materials but the impact of the BFI on the majority of secondary schools was slight until its recent policy changes. Now it is certainly a driving force in media education. In other words the earlier concentration in schools on film for its own sake had a very limited effect, played only a slight role in the growth of Media Studies and even less in encouraging media education. The nature of publications like *Screen* and *Screen Education* was such that they may have even discouraged an interest in media education in English teachers in particular. These journals addressed themselves to theory in a manner suitable chiefly for specialists in higher education, giving the impression, whether intentional or not, that their debates did not invite those on the 'lower' levels to join in.

The more recent development of a new organization called Film Education shows that there may yet be a better basis for special attention to film in schools. This initiative has produced materials for direct use by teachers in the classroom either related to films of current interest or about concepts concerning film. These materials have been mainly targeted at English teachers and the National Curriculum in English has provided a further stimulus for such work.

The advent of video has mean that film can be used with great precision by teachers and so the possibility of really close study exists more meaningfully than ever before. English teachers can use film in a variety of ways so as to prepare pupils for really detailed work in Media Studies but also as developing viewers. A class may read and study a film in its entirety, using it as the sole and sufficient text, considering all the key questions outlined above. Equally a class might take Kenneth Branagh's *Henry V* and compare it with Olivier's Second World War film of the play, considering not only the original play and the newer texts but also the relationship of each to changing historical circumstances. In order to do this a teacher might simply select extracts from each text to focus on the concepts that seem most relevant. What could take English teaching into more challenging areas would be the study of film in relation to other texts in, for example, the timing of a film within television schedules; or the circumstances of censorship concerning some films.

Video

The impact of video technology on all aspects of life, including life in school, is enormous if, as yet, undocumented. For our purposes it is worth setting out some basic points. The video has given the teacher highly sophisticated control of pupils' viewing and I shall return to this point. Recent legislation means that the teacher can record almost anything from television to show to a class, providing nearly unlimited access to all kinds of programmes for all teachers but, in particular, for the media teacher. For a small cost the teacher can hire any number of prerecorded videos to use in the classroom. Despite the fact that these points are well known in school by teachers of all subjects little has as yet been done to make the most of the learning potential offered by video.

The point about control is the most important. At present the great majority of video use in school is simply to show a programme, either in its entirety or in parts over a series of lessons. In other words the medium is used transparently, as if transmitting information straight to the viewer. It is evident that such use can be paralleled to the use of printed text in most subjects. In such circumstances, however, pupils need constantly to be reminded that such viewing is not 'natural'. Just as in their English lessons pupils would constantly carry out close reading of a variety of texts so they need to use the same approach with video. One of the simplest but strongest arguments for media education is that there is no necessary relationship between pupils watching a great deal and an increase in the sophistication that they bring to such viewing. In order to develop their competence as viewers as quickly as possible they need to have their attention drawn to the way in which media texts operate. It may well be that a number of teachers in a variety of subjects, by using video, can help in developing this competence. However, the English teacher needs to be the most active in such work, constantly using the technology of the video player to help pupils 'see' more exactly what has been used in the construction of a media text.

Radio

Radio is an underused medium, presumably because for most pupils, and many teachers, it is chiefly a source of music. As a result pupils tend to be less knowledgeable about radio in general and often associate any programming that is not mainly popular music with a dull worthiness. However, as there is a distance between most pupils and the great majority of radio so there is a great deal of potential in the medium. Pupils start with fewer preconceptions as well as less knowledge and they also have to concentrate extremely hard simply to absorb what is happening. This is a very rich area for the English teacher and I shall provide a fuller example of work.

Books

One of the ironies of secondary school English for many pupils is that they spend a great deal of time working with books without ever considering how the books themselves have been produced. I suspect that many pupils do retain a certain awe of books, although they may retain no interest in them, because of the mystique about books' origins that is never dispelled. English teachers are part of the conspiracy to build the magical aura of the author, that extraordinary creative genius who is, apparently, the sole producer of the holy text. I obviously exaggerate, but there is inevitably a paradox between the English teacher's emphasis on the sanctity of the text and its precise meaning and the process of manufacture and consumption of the mass produced object itself. English teachers want pupils to revere good texts both mentally and physically and so they want those pupils to feel the author's power present in the room and so do I. There is, however, no contradiction between developing pupil's admiration and respect for authors and their books and encouraging the same pupils to understand that books come into being because there is a profit-generating industry that produces them.

Perhaps many teachers might still argue that the process of publishing is of little interest to them or their pupils. I would have to say that such an attitude is not only wrong but it actually undermines the very edifice that they are trying to build; keeping the origins of books mysterious and somehow élitist does not promote a life-long interest in reading them. I would argue for the same spiral approach to understanding about publishing as for other aspects of media work. In other words pupils can begin to appreciate how a book is produced when they are in primary school and might leave secondary school with some grasp of the sophisticated process of the publishing industry. English teachers might well contribute valuably to pupils' economic and industrial understanding through such work. I shall discuss this idea in more depth in Chapter 7, when considering popular fiction.

Comics, magazines and the press

Of all aspects of the media, these three are almost certainly the most commonly worked on in English at present. Classrooms are full of pupils writing their own newspapers and producing magazines together. They are even occasionally allowed to read real examples too. I would not criticize such work in itself because it is a part of a broad movement to give pupils far more range in their writing and to help them understand the relationship between words in the abstract and text and illustration on the page. What I am suggesting is that more work on, for example, newspapers is not necessarily any more developmental than more work on the apostrophe; pupils may simply be repeating work with less interest and no increase in understanding. English departments have the central role in making their pupils fully literate and sophisticated readers of all texts but they have an especially vital job to do in educating future citizens about the nature of daily, weekly and monthly sources of information and pleasure.

Much of the earlier work on this aspect of the media in the 1950s and 1960s was carried out in the spirit of discriminate and resist; I do not need to define that in any more detail. Over the last 20 years the increase in attention to the press in particular has led to a far more open approach. However, before commenting on this broader approach, it is important to make a point through an example. For some reason many English teachers have continued to feel that one job they should attempt is the lifting of the tabloid veil from their pupils' eyes. They have felt that it would be relatively easy to cajole their classes into recognizing that the most popular tabloids were really rather silly comics but with a highly dangerous message. This patronizing and dismissive approach is in itself highly dangerous and silly. It simply alienates pupils from their teachers, not least because it implies that whoever reads such stuff – i.e. for many pupils, their parents – must be stupid. It also implies that the pupils and their friends are stupid and have no idea about the silliness of the papers in question.

The whole enterprise begins with the absurd assumption that no one should read such papers and that this generation of school leavers, will, of course, have been educated to be above such reading. The facts are very obviously different. If English teachers want pupils to understand that tabloids have all the contradictory elements of all newspapers – e.g. truth/lies, nonsense/serious news, objectivity/bias, racial tolerance/racism, anti-sexism/ sexism – then they have a far more challenging and necessarily systematic job to do. Essentially we should return to our key questions and the selection of any one indicates that subtlety and sophistication are needed, not a patron- izing bludgeon. It is in aspects of media work such as this that English departments have to question their existing practice very closely indeed.

The broadening out process mentioned above makes such questioning very timely. Departments have begun to place more emphasis on considering other kinds of reading such as comics and teenage and specialist interest magazines. This new emphasis seems to have come partly from concerns about the general lack of reading undertaken by adolescents and also from the expansion of titles and interest in this area of reading. Perhaps because teachers have felt comparatively ignorant about these publications so they have been more cautious in their personal attitudes towards them. This caution has provided a greater opportunity for a mutually investigative approach to such reading and more respect towards pupils' interests. I shall return to this area for discussion of some practical examples in Chapter 7.

Printed materials

There is a constant worry amongst those in authority about the domination of audiovisual texts over printed texts. One of the ironies in this worry is that there has never been such a proliferation of printed materials as we have now. 'Printed materials' is a catchall term but a very valuable one because it allows us to consider pamphlets, leaflets, circulars, junk mail, posters, pack- aging, labels, signs, badges, clothes and so on. There might be a temptation to dismiss all this ephemera as merely that; however, this would be an appalling waste of an otherwise rich source of interest and potential understanding. What is most important here is to return to the concern expressed at the beginning of the chapter. How can we make sense of all this? How can we approach such proliferation in any meaningful way? The answer is that we do need to have some approaches that make sense but that are in themselves open to questioning and revision. We need some theory, but theory that is neither rigid nor dogmatic.

4 English teaching and media theory

English teaching and 'theory'

As I have already argued, media education belongs chiefly within English in the secondary curriculum and earlier chapters have to some degree been devoted to providing the necessary rationale for this view. It is impossible to draw on any single, definitive theory of English as a secondary subject on which to base my view as the subject itself contains so many conflicting voices. I have given my own simple definition in Chapter 1 and this is certainly close to the Cox model entitled 'Cultural Analysis': 'A "Cultural Analysis" view emphasizes the role of English in helping children towards a critical understanding of the world and cultural environment in which they live. Children should know about the processes by which meanings are conveyed, and about the ways in which print and other media carry values' (DES 1989: 2.20–2.27). The Cox Report avoids the issue of favouring one theory underpinning English as a school subject by identifying five current, distinct strands without expressing particular support for any one.

In contrast to English, Media Studies has suffered from what might be termed an excess of theory (for discussions of this excess see Buckingham 1990a,b, Inglis 1990, Goodwyn 1991a) and the practical considerations of working with students have only recently made an impact on the field of Media Study. I shall not be arguing in any way from an anti-theoretical basis but will attempt to explain why the profusion of ideas and theories in Media Studies has rarely been applied for practical purposes in educational terms. For example, collections of essays such as *Media, Culture and Society* (Collins *et al.* 1986) and *The Media Reader* (Alvarado and Thompson 1990) are excellent sources of theory and analyses of the media but it would not be the intention of the writers or editors of such compilations to speak directly to secondary teachers. A more useful starting point would be *The Media Studies Book* (Lusted 1991) as this text is aimed specifically at teachers.

One of the long-term benefits of media education working within English may be that issues of theory, often highly problematic for the majority of English teachers and therefore usually marginalized, will become more central and more seriously analysed. This chapter aims to examine media theory from the English teacher's point of view. The examination is therefore deliberately partial and, in places, tentative. I hope to give some general insights into media theory and to suggest ways that these concepts may be applied within media education and in English teaching more generally. The implications of accepting these concepts goes a great deal further than media education itself and certainly much further than the rather restricted suggestions about media education in the original National Curriculum document (DES 1989: Chapter 9).

Mass media theory

The study of the mass media and its effects belongs within a range of domains – sociology and psychology continuing as the principal fields – and it has long been a major subject in its own right, especially in American higher education. There are now a range of degree and other tertiary level courses available in the United Kingdom, the BFI has provided some useful guides, for example, *Media Studies at 16+* (Blanchard 1989), *Media Education in Britain: An Outline* (BFI 1989) and *Adult Education Film Courses* (Cook 1988). The importance of mass media theory has, however, an important relationship to English teaching. I do not intend to provide a history of mass media theory, this has been very well covered elsewhere (for example Gurevitch *et al.* 1982), but instead to examine concepts that have a powerful role to play within English and media education. I have also tried to cover the initial responses of Leavis and Thompson to media influences. Their whole thrust from the late 1930s into the 1960s was to bolster the susceptible individual against the onslaught of the mass media (see Chapter 2).

The central point to make here is that this attitude to the mass media in the 1930s was shared by many and was extraordinarily homogeneous. As Gurevitch *et al.* express it: 'To a remarkable extent, there was a broad consensus during the inter-war period – to which many researchers, writing from a "right" as well as "left" perspective subscribed – that the mass media exercised a powerful and persuasive influence' (Gurevitch *et al.* 1982: 11). However, while Leavis and others continued in a sense, through their books and their journal *Scrutiny*, to promote this view, academic theory moved rapidly away from it. In what Gurevitch calls 'a new academic orthodoxy' the studies of the 1950s and 1960s suggested 'that the mass media have only a very limited influence' (Gurevitch *et al.* 1982: 12); it is interesting to note how Richard Hoggart's seminal *The Uses of Literacy* (1957) is quoted in support of this latter view by Murdock and Phelps (1973: 39). The views of Leavis and Thompson remained highly influential but they were not themselves subject to any influences or new ideas, least of all from the field of media theory.

In trying to explain the longevity of the Leavis/Thompson line it is important to recognize that the English teachers of the 1950s and 1960s and, to an extent, ever since, have been neurotically fascinated by advertising. A brief survey of Thompson's work in particular illustrates this and there are any number of examples of work related to advertising in English textbooks. Most of the examples seem to derive their rationale from sources like Vance Packard's *The Hidden Persuaders* (1957), based on research in the 1950s, in which pupils are encouraged to recognize the clever duplicities of the advertisers and are shown how to withstand the seductive ploys used to ensnare them.

Essentially, by concentrating not on media but on a range of texts invented to sell products, English teachers dug a kind of mental foxhole from which they could take occasional pot shots against that they saw as the impending assault. Teaching about advertising seemed to make sense, because of advertising's universality and its specific focus on selling, but in fact such teaching was a kind of chimera. You could demonstrate any number of points about advertising by studying advertising but you could rarely get beyond its own, quite narrow, limitations. One of the greatest ironies of this obsession with advertising is that, paradoxically, it offered the evidence of its own limitations. Advertising does increase sales but there is no formulaic principle which means that there is a logical and explicable relationship between mass advertising and massive sales. The individual adult consumer (and school pupil) remains remarkably unimpressed given the range of advertising apparently pressing in on the consciousness. The concentration on advertising was a dead end.

Mass media theory continued to exert a kind of influence on English teaching right through the 1970s and 1980s but this influence was more or less a hangover from previous generations. In the field of media theory itself the new, post World War Two orthodoxy was once more challenged in a way that might seem to support the omnipotent media idea and thus to justify the resistant approach of many teachers; however, as I shall show, this challenge contained heterogeneous and competing views.

The Marxist position continued to posit, as had the Frankfurt School in the 1930s, the existence of a vastly influential media machine on the basis of its ideological configurations (see, for example, Marcuse 1972). From this viewpoint the media sanctioned, supported and actively promoted the continuing domination of the currently powerful classes. These views were not based on empirical research on audiences, indeed such research in Marxist terms could only be absurd, as the audiences, by the nature of their false consciousness, would be unable to detect the ideological forces controlling them. Meanwhile the liberal, humanist tradition was resisting such empirically unsupported theorizing by specific studies which tended to show how little influence the media had to change an audience's views.

It has been suggested (Gurevitch *et al*. 1982: Chapter 1) that these two apparently opposing positions are practically aligned. Empirical studies often show not only that media have failed to change audience views but also that they have had a reinforcing effect on currently dominant positions. Inevitably the empirical studies have contained their own ideological and theoretical positions however much they may have claimed to be without them. The two basic views, liberal humanist and Marxist, are actually complementary.

Where does this leave the English teacher with a classroom of pupils to work with? The first conclusion it seems to me is a pragmatic one and that is to make sure there is no one remaining in the advertising foxhole. Media education is far more insightful and valuable when the teacher begins from a considered and cautious position; pupils are surrounded by advertising but that proves nothing in itself. Second, both the Marxist and the liberal positions on mass media influence suggest that the media are powerful but not in simple, obvious ways. In order to get at the genuine nature of media influence and its meanings a teacher must raise questions about dominant societal and cultural views. Such views cannot suddenly become known. The process will be gradual, the progress may be erratic. A teacher and a department will need a systematic, coherent but necessarily flexible and contextualized approach. The third point is that the teacher needs to locate his or her personal theory in order to recognize the way in which it must inform teaching. There are suggestions about how a department might question its own theory and practice in Chapter 8.

Media education and theory

Media education in schools has existed in practice partly in English and partly in specialist areas like Film Studies, Communications and Media Studies. Most ideas about media education have come from these latter areas and certainly the theoretical underpinning for media education has not come from within English. The National Curriculum documents concerning English have borrowed their ideas chiefly from recent BFI publications, most notably *Primary Media Education: A Curriculum Statement* (Bazalgette 1989). A crucial and ironic link in the development of media education as separated from Media Study can be traced to the work of Leavis and Thompson.

The attention given by Leavis and Thompson to the media and their cry to resist their influence inaugurated media-related activities in the secondary school (see Masterman 1985). Equally as media technology developed so the opportunity to study the media increased. The result was that enthusiasts took up the teaching of film and eventually Media Studies and so these

became separate and distinct areas in the secondary school. As these specialist areas were developing in school so the various debates about media theory
were continuing; there was always a consistently close relationship between
media theory and ideas about specialist Media Study practice in schools; the
influence of *Screen* and *Screen Education* seem to have been considerable
(Buckingham 1990b).

In English, when debates were raging in the universities about struc-
turalism, post-structuralism and so on (see, for example, *Re-Reading English*
(Widdowson 1982) and *Rewriting English* (Batsleer *et al.* 1985)), there was
almost no evidence that these literary debates had any perceptible influence
on secondary English teaching. A small debate was conducted in the pages of
The English Magazine, for example No. 10 'The Poststructuralist Always
Reads Twice' (Exton 1983), No. 15 'The Subject of Literature' (Eagleton
1985) and in other journals such as *English in Education*. Debates in English
have circled endlessly around the possible reform of English A Level but
actual changes have been few (Greenwell 1987). In a volume like *Dialogue
and Difference* (Brooker and Humm 1989), which claims to investigate
English in secondary, higher and further education, there are only three
essays out of 15 which fully concentrate on secondary English teaching; the
essays are 'Never mind English: this is theory in the secondary school', 'I see
the murderer is a skilful door opener: investigating autobiography and detec-
tive stories with 11 to 18 year olds' and 'Changing literature at "A" level'.

One book of the last few years that addresses 'new' literary theory in
relation to English teaching *Literary Theory and English Teaching* (Griffith
1987) is an attempt, and a very successful one, to introduce teachers to new
theories and to illuminate their pedagogical potential; it does not attempt
to describe any existing practice or claim that it already exists. Many of the
theories and approaches outlined by Griffith, however, complement the
definition of English that I am currently proposing. A fascinating American
book, aimed mainly at English teachers in higher education in the USA, is
Textual Power (Scholes 1985). In this text Scholes posits an argument very
close to my own '. . . we must stop "teaching literature" and start "studying texts". Our rebuilt apparatus [English] must be devoted to textual
studies . . . Our favourite works of literature need not be discarded. All kinds
of texts, visual as well as verbal, polemical as well as seductive, must be
taken as the occasions for further textuality.' The 'new' literary theories can
certainly play a part in broadening the definition of English in secondary
school but their impact is still relatively slight and inevitably we are drawn
back to media theory.

The media education theory of importance for current teachers began to
develop in the 1970s and it is expounded very clearly in a number of recent
publications (Bazalgette 1989, Buckingham 1990b, Bowker 1991). The most
seminal text of the 1980s was Masterman's *Teaching the Media*, first published in 1985. It is the key text for a number of reasons but in particular

because it was the first full-length study which tried to relate academic media theory to classroom practice.

The media education theory of the 1970s still tended to identify the audience, and so also the pupil, as passive and susceptible. Teachers, who accepted this view, had to force their pupils' eyes open. The pedagogic approach had therefore to be authoritarian and didactic, students had to be told what and how to think about the repressive powers of media institutions. However, teachers working on Film courses or, later, Media Studies courses, were perfectly aware that pupils were far from passive consumers, slavishly following the dominant ideology. The result of such teaching was that far-reaching questions were asked about how media education, rather than instruction, could be possible if it derived its practice from such rigid and dogmatic theory.

The influence of Masterman

One response to this difficulty was Len Masterman's book *Teaching the Media*. It succeeded and to a large extent made rather obsolete his earlier work *Teaching About Television*. This former text concentrates on television as the key medium for society generally and education in particular. However the second book repudiates this approach insisting that media education must not isolate any particular medium but must endeavour to give pupils a comprehensive understanding of the media in general.

Masterman's work has been, rightly, highly influential and his second book remains the most powerful and coherent argument for media education that we have. My brief discussion does not try to do justice to either his books or his influence; I am simply concerned here with key points that apply to the present and future development of media education in relation to English.

One significant point is that *Teaching the Media* provides us with a very useful insight into the struggle between the nature of media theory and the nature of teaching and learning. Masterman's basic concept of the media contains a number of key strands. First, he is close to the Leavis and Marxist views in positing a media establishment whose effect is to support and generally promote the capitalist status quo. Second, one of his principal aims is to help pupils become more critical and resistant viewers. Third, his pedagogical approach to achieve this aim is to attempt to abolish the teacher as an authority figure and to create a non-hierarchical classroom. This results in some problems in, for example, his section on discussion where the teacher is left with a comradely role, as far as possible alongside the pupils; such classroom activity, deriving its pedagogic style from Paolo Freire, is termed dialogue. The tension here is that the teacher does know more about what is going on in the media but has to withhold this knowledge to let the pupils find out for themselves.

I am entirely in sympathy with the principles underlying this approach but they posit a situation which I recognize as entirely unrealistic at present. What Masterman, and others, point out is that pupils know a great deal about the media simply from their own interests and exposure at home. It is not patronizing to suggest that such knowledge may be chiefly implicit and inactive, possibly inert. The teacher makes a number of decisions about the material and ideas to be considered in the classroom; subsequent decisions need to be made about the discussion and, this being the key point, what can move that discussion on. Naturally the teacher makes many mistakes, this is learning; but experience and trust in the human ability to be motivated and interested mean that the teacher's pressure on the discussion need not be anything but developmental.

Much of Masterman's specific attention is focused on the non-fictional, documentary aspects of the media. The majority of his suggestions for practical work are centred around the news and other informative aspects of media output; this seems to stem from a desire to give status and credibility to the serious study of the media, to avoid the taint of entertainment at all costs. One of the chief difficulties with this emphasis on the news and so on is that however worthy it is, it neglects and potentially excludes vast areas of media experience which are the predominant interest of the majority of pupils. It also differentiates media study from a subject like English which gives great scope to entertainments like fiction, drama and poetry.

As I indicated earlier, Masterman is essentially hostile to English teachers as the principal providers of media education. This hostility is curious. Masterman's pedagogic approach, it seems to me, is borrowed from progressive English teaching. Such an approach places the experience of each pupil at the centre of the learning model, putting great emphasis on the developmental aspects of language use and giving the teacher the role more of organizer and facilitator than teacher. The question raised but unanswered by this approach is how understanding about the media is to be properly developed in the secondary school if this is the only learning model in operation. Is the alternative for every teacher to become a media theorist and so, in his or her small way, to add to the pupil's rapidly developing knowledge? We know that the pupil's knowledge about language may be increased across the curriculum but it is not fully developed without the coherent centre of English.

I would like to see all teachers extending pupil's understanding and enjoyment of the media, as I would their enjoyment and understanding of language and reading. However, whether all teachers achieve this or not, there still needs to be a focus, a place in which concepts and their consequences are considered in proper depth.

The work of Masterman has been enormously influential in the 1980s and has certainly developed thinking about media education throughout all phases of the education system. Much of the most recent important work is either a development of his ideas or a reaction against them leading to a new position. The now distant but crucial thesis of Leavis and Thompson, the antithesis of Masterman have now, paradoxically, produced some kind of synthesis: a synthesis that is finally bringing together the English and the media specialist.

The coming of media education

Since the late 1980s the most important developments in the thinking about media education have been brought together by the BFI's education section and have been summed up in their two *Curriculum Statements* (Bazalgette 1989, Bowker 1991). These collections are certainly far more important than the few paragraphs devoted to media education in the National Curriculum documents. It is vital to examine the basic theory of media education outlined in the documents and to relate it to good practice in English teaching.

The underlying rationale for media education itself builds on much previous work. It is undeniable that the mass media are dominant factors in all our lives and that this dominance is increasing. Children and young people are especially avid consumers of media texts. Inevitably most of this consumption takes place outside school hours and is not legitimized as part of education in any formal sense. However, media technology is increasingly in evidence in all phases of education as a part of the learning process. The messages that these media provide cannot be simplistically disengaged from the media that carry them; in order to understand the full meaning of any media message one must have some understanding of the medium itself. Media education theory, based on the above rationale is relatively simple and comprehensible; this is my version, but it draws heavily on the BFI materials.

Understanding about the media can be progressively developed but such development, like that of competence in the various modes of language, is not linear. It is best represented as a widening spiral, the individual may constantly return to key concepts and each time may increase understanding. It is not therefore a hierarchical model in which one concept precedes another.

This model is in principle value free, that is, it does not attempt to erect a hierarchy of values that will establish a canon of texts. However the individual's ability to make personal judgements is enhanced and extended by the nature of the descriptive and analytic processes involved in comprehending the media.

It is a model that integrates thinking and doing, i.e. it does not say that there is only an abstract theory which can be absorbed, instead it insists on learners developing understanding by analysing and by working in different media. This emphasis on practice does not mean that pupils have to simulate professional standards of production but to reach towards an understanding of what such practices consist of. In this way media education has moved away from a media study, mass media theory approach and towards an approach much more typical of an English classroom. In English one of the most notable developments over the century, made concrete by coursework in the GCSE and now some A Level, is the move away from the passive, merely appreciative pupil, to the active, productive, reflective individual. In simple terms, pupils in English read professional and amateur writers but also write themselves and publish their own work.

Getting hold of the media

How do we help pupils to get hold of something as vast and as amorphous as the media (see the definition in Chapter 3)? The synthesis that I mentioned above (see p. 47) is not definitive but has provided us with a means of encapsulating the media and subjecting it to rigorous analysis. I shall now follow the terminology of the BFI documents, providing my own explanations and drawing attention to links with existing English practice. The key areas of knowledge and understanding are media agencies, media categories, media technologies, media languages, media audiences and media representations (Bazalgette 1989: 7–20, Bowker 1991: 1–17, Grahame 1991: 10–20.)

Agencies

Historically, English teachers have tended to accept texts as they are (see Chapter 3) and to direct pupils' attention to them as relatively unproblematic objects; their argument might be summarized as follows: pupils should learn to appreciate the quality of the text, recognize the skill of the author and agree with the given, critically accepted interpretation/s. This very narrow view suggests that a text is simply produced by an author and read by readers, little or no consideration is given to the actual production and distribution of the printed text. A media text highlights the simplistic basis for such an assumption. Neither teacher nor pupil need much detailed knowledge to recognize the complexities of media production. A film provides a striking example. The relationship between 'author' and viewer does have a real comparison with writer/reader but equally there is a parallel between the fact that, under normal circumstances, literally hundreds of people have played a part in creating a film and a considerable number have been instrumental in publishing and distributing a book. It always seems quite easy to say who wrote the book, giving the author the essential responsibility for the final product; the author, even the *auteur*, of a film is much harder to specify even when the director takes the credit.

The teacher's role is to problematize the pupils' assumptions in relation to all texts. There is a degree of technical knowledge that might be used in such work but it is certainly not essential; it is perhaps more appropriate within Media Studies. What the teacher needs is to push pupils into questioning how a text has been produced. The key question is 'Who is communicating and why?' as this is a fiendishly complicated question to answer, part of the necessary understanding for pupils is just to gain a sense of that complexity. One important teaching approach will not be to 'appreciate' the complexity but to demystify it.

Developing pupils' understanding means considering not only key individuals who made the text such as, in the case of a film, writer, director, actors, technical staff and so on but also financiers, distributors and advertisers. Any controversial film highlights issues of censorship and control. With television texts the whole range of corporate issues are involved including the role of the government and even that of other nations; a good example of a text at the centre of a struggle between a number of agencies is the documentary about the deaths of three IRA members, *Death on the Rock*.

To some teachers this idea of agencies may immediately ring old alarm bells. There may be a feeling of irrelevance, a worry that all this is just a distraction from the 'text' and that with books you are on much more solid and safe ground. I think that this idea of agencies must have its place in English generally. Can there be any doubt that a pupil/student studying Shakespeare ought to know about the circumstances in which the plays were produced? It seems to me to increase Shakespeare's achievement considerably to know about the kind of theatre he worked in and the audience that he wrote for. The question is more to do with: when can pupils gain from such knowledge of Shakespeare? My personal answer would be chiefly at Key Stage 4, but that a beginning should be made to help pupils to enjoy the plays (in whatever form) as early as possible. This point holds true for all work with literature. At present pupils are regularly asked to reflect on why an author produced a text and on what the meanings of that text may be, but rarely on how that text comes to be, literally, in the classroom. One of the great opportunities provided by media education is that it helps pupils to see that agencies are involved in the production of all texts.

Categories

One of the most crucial areas for teachers and pupils is the question of categorizing. It is always a challenge to teach about form in the English lesson. As Robert Protherough's research about story (Hayhoe and Parker 1990) has shown, forms are rarely interrogated but usually pupil knowledge is assumed. The assumption is that because a term, like 'story' or 'character', may be quite familiar pupils will have a clear sense of how to use it. In Protherough's research on 'story' he demonstrates that this key term story is taken absolutely for granted by teachers as understood by all pupils but in fact it is a highly problematic concept. The research also shows how the difficulty of definition is part of the fascination and interest of working with stories for teachers and pupils alike. Only when forms like the sonnet or the ballad are being introduced do English teachers feel the need to provide a precise, contextualized definition. I am not suggesting that lessons should constantly bore pupils with involved investigations of form but media categories illustrate what a productive areas this can be. Questioning the definition of a form and testing the definition with practical examples is a very effective way of deepening understanding.

There are several types of media category to consider, the first category being the different media themselves, i.e. television, radio and so on. I have considered this range at length above (see Chapter 3). All pupils need to develop an understanding of the nature of these categories, the freedoms and constraints that they offer, the particular kinds of communicative power that they contain. It is also worth stressing that whenever a teacher, or a pupil, asks the question, 'What would this text be like in a different medium?', then potentially fascinating and sophisticated issues are raised. These issues can only be dealt with at a high level if pupils' implicit knowledge is made explicit through discussion, analysis and practical work.

The second category is media forms: easily recognizable examples are documentary, serials and news. These are broad areas that often span, and can be compared across, a number of media. Equally these forms can be linked to and explored alongside literary and other texts. Documentary is a good instance. Pupils can learn about the act of documenting from considering writers' attempts to record and objectify experience alongside the work of film and documentary makers. All forms are structured through traditions and conventions that allow for compliance and departure from the norm. Media forms provide excellent sources for developing pupils' understanding of conventions and structures, this knowledge can be complemented and extended by comparison with written texts.

The third and most specific category is genres, this may also be the richest for teachers and English teachers in particular. The list of examples is potentially endless: in films (horror, western, disaster, war); on television (soap opera, quiz shows, chat shows, situation comedies); magazines (women's, teenage, comics, hobbies, etc.). Considering these genres leads teacher and pupils into a full exploration of not just what a text means but also how it means. The key question is 'What kind of text is it?' and this raises all kinds of definitional concerns, particularly when a text crosses boundaries such as a drama–documentary or deliberately breaks and plays with them, as *Twin Peaks* plays with soap-opera conventions.

Technologies

This area has as much to do with meaning as with sophisticated technology. The important issue to consider is how something was produced and what difference that makes to its meaning. A pair of scissors, used to crop a picture, is an example of technology changing meaning; the use of a wide-angle lens to photograph a demonstration is an example of technology influencing meaning; the use of a computer to adjust the background of an image is an example of the latest technology determining meaning. In a sense these are only the most obvious examples because they are visible actions taken using a specific piece of technology. Far more subtle but just as important are questions like what difference does having a camera make to the history of your family? Or, if you were producing the highlights of a particular event, what would you edit out and what would you keep? In this way some knowledge of what technology can do, whether you have it available or not, allows pupils to explore imaginative possibilities.

The use of technology brings with it questions about the extent to which pupils can learn from direct experience, from 'hands on'. One fear that some English teachers may have is that they, the supposed experts, lack technical expertise and that their school also lacks the necessary equipment. Of course, it can be highly beneficial for teachers and pupils if a school has the latest equipment but the possession of such equipment is not the most vital issue. Pupils can learn a great deal without ever using a video camera or a desk top publishing program. What they need is a practical task that makes them reflect on how the technology in use offers both ways of meaning and, potentially, limits other ways. The selection of a technology is the first of a series of choices in any attempt to create a meaning or meanings. What teachers should definitely avoid is leading pupils into the production of materials that they are ultimately disappointed with because the product is 'not like the real thing'.

English teachers can draw on their well-established practice of encouraging pupils to produce real writing for a real audience without iniquitous comparisons to professional materials.

Languages

Language here is used in the sense that every medium has its own codes and conventions that are like a language which has to be learned. Once the lauguage is well known both the makers and the receivers can play with its conventions and produce sophisticated meanings. Media codes and conventions are also like a first language in that each individual has plenty of implicit knowledge of the language but may lack the competence to utilize such knowledge in an explicit way.

In studying the media the teacher has to problematize the nature of media language because pupils may feel that they understand what is being conveyed yet lacking any explicit sense of where this understanding comes from. They are reading a media text without an actual awareness of how, or even that they are, reading. If you show pupils ten extracts of ten seconds each from ten quite different television programmes they will have a great deal to say about them; how can this be? It can only be because they have read the extracts and picked up on the codes and conventions being used and so are able to draw on their extensive existing knowledge of media categories and media language. They may be able to tell a great deal about what is happening in a television drama without seeing the screen if they can simply hear the music; the codings of music are highly specialized but also extremely conventional during most programmes. It is an excellent exercise for pupils to watch a minute of any programme with the sound turned down and to predict what the sound consists of.

Within any media context, language, in the more ordinary sense of human speech and writing, is operating in very special ways. Pupils have a great deal of implicit knowledge about the use of language within the media. There are very few pupils who cannot recognize the style of *The Sun*, who cannot tell when a radio speaker is a DJ or who do not appreciate that there is a particular form of speech for newsreaders on the major television channels. It is an indication of the potential of media education to consider that different levels of reflection and analysis might be brought to describing the language (in terms of speech and codes) of television news by pupils in Key Stages 2, 3 and 4. No pupil could be said to have acquired much useful knowledge about language if he or she left school without detailed consideration of the power of language as used in and by the media.

Audiences

The whole concept of audience is one that ought to appeal powerfully to all English teachers. I use 'ought' deliberately because one of the most far-reaching changes in English teaching over the years and the 1980s in particular has been the broad acceptance of the need to find real audiences for pupils' work, whether written or oral. The English teacher may have held on to providing the trusted adult role for pupils' writing but has probably also sought out a whole range of audiences from younger pupils to old age pensioners in order to give authenticity and purpose to the work of a class (see, for example, the materials produced by The National Writing Project). A considerable amount of emphasis in the oral component of English is directed towards audience and individual listener awareness.

What media education provides is an opportunity to extend very considerably pupils' understanding of audience; in some instances it may easily be the best place to introduce the idea itself. There are a number of inter-related points to consider. First, all media producers are highly concerned about their audience; whether an editor of a tabloid or the producer of *The Archers*, both have an existing audience to consider and to try and keep. This, mainly idealized audience will have, according to those producers, certain characteristics. At any time pupils can analyse what the audience for any media text is supposed to be and what it actually is. If a particular soap opera is the most popular at present it is quite easy to find out if such popularity is reflected in the age group of the class in question. Whatever the initial answer the more interesting question – why? – follows almost automatically.

Second, what makes up an audience, how is it constructed? All pupils can reflect on the nature of a text and speculate, drawing on a wide range of existing knowledge, about how a text is trying to create and sustain its audience. Here, at least, advertising is a rich source of interest. Who is a particular advertisement aimed at, how is it supposed to affect its intended audience, is there any way of finding out if an advertisement is effective?

Third, how can you match a text to its audience in terms of a special interest? With television, for example, what assumptions are programme makers displaying by scheduling soap operas at particular times? What comments do DJs make during their programmes and what does this suggest about who they think is listening? Are the audiences for tabloids and broadsheet papers entirely different species or is there much more to readers than such simple distinctions suggest?

Fourth, the class itself, a group within the class, an individual within the class, all these are audiences. This particular audience has all the raw material for audience research, i.e. it is supposed to have a great deal in common, similar ages, same school, likely to come from roughly the same urban, suburban or rural area, certainly the same region, yet it will not provide, despite powerful public peer pressure, a homogeneous response. In other words the meanings created by the various individuals about any text will differ very considerably. This point may be especially important for some teachers who might feel that the rich potential of a challenging literary text is quite distinct from any apparently ephemeral media text. Meaning can always be worked on and even a seemingly simple media text, *Tom and Jerry* perhaps, takes a great deal of explaining. A GSCE group could have a very sophisticated discussion not only about how the cartoon is supposed to please its intended audience but also about what meanings that audience might make from the programme, comparing these meanings with their own.

Representations

My last point about the nature of meaning leads on to an absolutely essential aspect of media education, representation. Whatever *Tom and Jerry* is supposed to show, what does it actually show? How, for example, are women and black people represented when they feature on the cartoon and does this representation matter? If so, to whom does it matter? Audience and representation are, inevitably, closely bound up.

Representation is paradoxically the most difficult and the most obvious concept to deal with. It is 'obvious' because once pupils have grasped even a basic sense of the meaning of representation they can never go back to the time of not knowing; however, knowledge can hover on the edge of understanding for a long, possibly indefinite time.

For example, to many adults as well as children, the television news simply seems to show the world as it is; it seems a window on that world. The newscasters themselves claim to be part of such an instrument, everything about the programme is serious but suitably slick and there are the pictures themselves, clear and incontrovertible. It is comparatively easy with a class of quite young pupils, say 11 year olds, to take the front pages of four different newspapers and help them see that the news on that particular day has had various interpretations. However, it is far more difficult to take a BBC news broadcast and to help pupils, even much older pupils, recognize the ideological construction of any particular item. Yet this is the challenge of media education for all teachers but especially for English teachers. No child should have to undertake a specialist Media Studies course to understand at least something about representation.

It is worth stressing at this point that I am not slipping into the media conspiracy view discussed earlier in the chapter. I am not positing a mass media audience of naïve readers or viewers who think that the media simply present texts, we all have some sense that reality is re-presented to us through these texts. I am concerned with a highly sophisticated audience whose reactions and interpretations are constantly shifting and evolving. What does an audience consider its reality to be and what relation does this bear to the media texts it reads? This sounds like a highly abstract question but it is simply evidence of the difficulty of grappling with representation. A sophisticated and experienced audience may find it much harder to see the nature of certain representations because of all their knowledge. It is, for example, much easier to speculate on the nature of representations in another country's media rather than in your own; the cultural distance provides the equivalent of the problematizing that I have referred to a number of times above.

Whether a text claims to be realistic or draws attention to its own artificiality, its audience decides what mediation of reality is present. A text re-presents the world in a number of particular ways. First there is the production of the text; who has produced it and for what purpose? Second, who is this text intended for, what expectations does it seem to engage? Third, how is the subject presented, what mode and context help to define its intended meanings? Fourth, what codes and conventions are embedded in the text for the audience to recognize and, usually, accept?

Representation raises all sorts of questions about ideology, hegemony, and stereotyping. Stereotyping is probably the issue closest to the concerns of most English teachers. Most teachers are conscious of sexism and racism in language generally and in literature particularly. However, stereotyping is always far more complex than it appears. Where it is often most obvious, for example, in the stereotyped representation of 'foreigners' in comedy, it is hardly likely to be a revelation to pupils that real foreign people are not actually like this. It is the insidious and subtle aspects of stereotyping that are most pernicious and require sensitive and sophisticated handling.

One way to get at the pervasiveness of certain societal values and basic ideologies such as attitudes to race is to analyse absence and marginalization rather than to hammer away at caricature stereotypes in soap operas. If pupils analyse programmes for what they ignore and look at schedules for what never seems to appear or, if it does, when it does, then they are being challenged far more genuinely to think about 'reality' as represented on the media. After such work they may come back to the more obvious stereotypes with far more rigour and real attention.

Any work on representations in the media brings in consideration of the five other areas in a complex and interrelated way. To ask pupils to consider how school and pupils are presented in, say, *Grange Hill* leads to considering who produces the programme (agencies) and who it is intended for (audiences)? Equally pupils will consider why it looks as it does, how is it that some shots look 'real' and others are clearly in a studio (categories, technology)? How does the programme work, does it contain serious issues or is it a comedy or both (categories, genre, language)? 'Is *Grange Hill* realistic in its representations of school and pupils?' The question of representation can only be properly attempted when serious consideration has been given to the full range of key areas.

Conclusion

The cumulative effect of reading about the six key areas in media education may be off-putting to some teachers. It may seem as if all classroom work in media education sounds fiercely analytical and hyper-serious. I hope that the next three chapters will show how exciting and enjoyable media-related English work can be. It is always the prerogative of the teacher to decide what terminology to use with pupils.

It is worth reiterating here that these six key areas were identified as the most important aspects of media education in the late 1980s. They are simply part of a developing basis for media education that at no point excludes or attempts to diminish pupils' enjoyment or personal response. For experienced or inexperienced English teachers these six, key areas, provide a way of planning and evaluating media education within English. They also provide a means of challenging and clarifying existing practice. An English department can think through how it may cover these media education areas, to what extent this coverage involves introducing new material or adapting and extending existing work. The key questions related to each area of media knowledge provide a precise way of raising issues about the broadest possible range of texts. Through such scrutiny it should be possible for a department to integrate media education and also to analyse how such integration can extend and develop existing good practice in English.

5 Integrating media education

In this chapter I shall explore the relationship that can exist between media education and the traditionally accepted key elements of English. I define the key elements at their most fundamental levels, that is the four modes Reading, Writing, Speaking and Listening. The other key division for English teachers is into literature and language. Most models of good practice are based on the principle that, for the majority of the time, the integration of the four modes is vital in the classroom. Most English lessons are not divided up into writing only or speaking only but operate a combination of these and the other two modes. However, as with the Attainment Targets of the National Curriculum and with GCSE assessment criteria, we need to separate the modes and also divide into language and literature when analysing and identifying what aspects and elements need to be covered and how and when this should happen; I shall look more closely at integrated activities in Chapter 8. For this reason I will look at reading and writing separately and speaking and listening together, all in relation to media education, placing literature within the reading section and reserving a brief, specific section for language. The concluding section looks at how media education can act as a bridge between English and the National Curriculum's cross-curricular themes.

Reading the media – audio-visual texts

The teaching of reading continues to be a topic, rather like the teaching of grammar, that ignites controversy whenever it is discussed and about which everyone has an opinion. In contrast the 'teaching of watching' or 'the teaching of listening' seem peculiar ideas to most people and certainly do not instigate controversy as yet. Of course the media produce almost as much print as audio-visual material but the former is, in a sense, taken care of within the print reading debate; I shall return therefore to print on p. 60.

As I discussed earlier (Chapter 1), Bazalgette points out (Potter 1990) that if children came to school with as much exposure to print as to television then many of them might already be functionally literate. The assumption is always made that watching and understanding is so much easier than reading and understanding; constant denigrating comparisons are made between the value of reading a book and the worthlessness of watching television. My immediate response to these comparisons is that they lack empirical proof and that they are made by partial judges, that is by people who place an absolute and profound faith in a print-based culture and whose accession to power and position has derived to a great extent from their ability to master print.

Amongst all this prejudice there are issues that deserve genuine attention. You can watch television or a film with only a part of your concentration and still retain a reasonable amount of a text's potential meanings; this seems much harder to do with print, skimming a written text, for example, is a deliberate and very precise strategy. Another point about media reading is that you can watch a film without any spoken language or where the speech is of an unknown language and still have a reasonable idea of what is happening; this makes watching seem simpler. Watching is often a social activity and therefore interrupted and potentially broken up, it can be a very different experience to the act of reading a print text. However, print reading is also far more of a public activity than we tend to think, many adults do most of their reading in transit, in waiting situations, at work and so on; many pupils do most or even all of their print reading in the very public arena of the classroom.

In order to reinforce this point about the tendency to underestimate the demands of watching it is worth examining in more depth the example of the film in an unknown language. In the flow of ordinary experience all our senses may be employed in interpreting the nature of any moment or event. All speakers of a language place a high degree of reliance on the speech around them to help interpret what is happening. When there is no speech, for whatever reason, the only other language available is the visual. This is not visual language in terms of the highly specialized codes of art but in human, societal terms, it is representative language. We read this language every second that our eyes are open. The vast majority of children are engaged in visual interpretation almost from the moment of birth. However much we come to rely on speech, and later writing, to understand our world, we continue to read visual signs. So children can learn to watch television and begin to value and enjoy its meanings because its correspondence is close, although it is not the same, as their own visual experience. Children could watch the film in an unknown language and interpret the making of meanings. This competence and the proximity of visual text to ordinary experience tend to disguise and obscure the complexity of the interpretive responses being made.

Any visual text has been encoded in a number of ways by its producers; the meanings it bears are various but the codings are there for the watcher to decode and make sense of. Some of the meanings, such as ideological messages, may be encoded without any conscious intention on the part of the producers (see Chapter 4). For the viewer these multifarious codings are all there but operating on a number of levels, many of them are not actively decoded but simply absorbed without any conscious effort. In this way the process is exactly like the decoding of a text, the difference may be that it is quite easy to call print a code and to see that the black marks on paper can be just that. However *The News* or *EastEnders* may appear somehow 'natural', their codes have to be teased out and made known.

The most effective approach to decoding has its nearest parallel in what English teachers call close reading. In media education the process is usually called denotation and connotation and there is no reason why teachers and pupils should not use these terms. If we think of a still image as perhaps the easiest form to work on then what the image denotes is exactly what the viewer sees. So a stereotypical and clichéd car advertisement might have a scantily dressed young woman stretched over the car's bonnet; that is all that one might describe as being visible in the picture. However the connotations of the image are evident; it seems likely that the image producers are suggesting that the car would provide its inevitably male owner with 'sex appeal'. There are many other encodings in such an image, whilst only some will be stereotypical they all need to be read very closely in order for the denoting and connoting to be effectively undertaken.

Denotation and connotation are terms whose currency derives partly from semiotics, the science of signs. The power of the sign in media images is another matter which complicates and intensifies media messages. In a sense every image is full of signs and these may be the principal means of its encoding. A well known series of cigarette advertisements which feature some slashed purple silk can only be explained in terms of the connotations of this sign. Semiotics offers a powerful way of decoding meanings from all aspects of the media.

For most English teachers close reading becomes practical criticism when pupils become A-Level students. This methodology still employs the techniques originially outlined by I.A. Richards in *Practical Criticism* (1929). However the fundamental concept that underpins practical criticism is one of hierarchical values. The technique is expected to help students reveal not so much the meaning of a text but its worth. In this way denotation and connotation offer a distinctly different approach. Using them students are enabled to recognize how the basic image or images are loaded with an ideology and its particular values. Their aesthetic and subjective judgement will be operating but it can be separated, to a large extent, from the analytic process itself.

In order to undertake close reading of specific forms such as types of poetry or different forms of prose pupils are expected to adopt an increasingly specialized vocabulary. Poetry is the most obvious example because its constructedness is apparent at the visual as well as linguistic level. An area that will become of increasing importance to English teachers will be the usefulness of the technical vocabulary of the media in developing pupils' understanding.

If pupils watch a brief excerpt from a film they will have an implicit understanding of its narrative. If they watch the extract again and attempt to count the number of technical operations that have occurred and attempt to name them they are likely to be surprised, first by the number and second by how much they know about these operations. It is likely that they may encounter close-ups, tracking shots, a camera panning over a scene, probably theme music and perhaps a voice-over. Camera angles will constantly change, perhaps several times in as many seconds. The pupils will have read much of this action on their first viewing and they will have missed at least some and possibly a great deal. It is not a question of 'getting it right'. As with a complex print text pupils can return at different ages and find far more than they once could. The English teacher can broaden and deepen understanding by the judicious use of technical terms as and when appropriate. Here seems to be an almost perfect analogy with knowing about language, most of the time terms are unnecessary but equally there are moments when their use can provide conceptual breakthroughs in knowledge that may last a lifetime. The teacher has as powerful and stimulating a role to play in such work as in any study of a poem, play or written story.

The understanding of media texts, their close reading, should be bound up with practical work in the same way that the reading of print texts is deepened by discussion and writing. There are many ways of achieving this integration and I offer here just a simple illustration, one that presumes that the teacher has access to an ordinary camera or two and to a video camera.

A class of whatever age might be asked, probably working in small groups to take a representative photograph of their school. It will not take long before the groups begin to feel the impossibility of such a task. 'Representative of what?' 'Who is this picture for?' 'How big can the picture be?' 'Would we really be allowed to take a picture of older pupils when they are smoking?' In a way the class need never take the picture in order to understand the implications of the concept of representation. However, the act of taking the picture and of seeing it developed will lead to a new dimension. There is a technical level to engage with, the competence, or otherwise of the photographers and the power or lack of it of the camera. More important in the long run is the likely wish to repeat the exercise and to improve on it, to attempt a second draft.

At any point an image of the school may be questioned and radically changed by placing under it or near it one or more works, anchoring the image. What difference does it make if the groups can select one word of these three: school, home or prison? What will the groups come up with if their chosen image is suddenly contextualized by being placed in a particular frame for which they must create an accompanying title such as the front cover of the school brochure, a teenage magazine article about truancy or a book about education for readers from another country?

Perhaps a class might work on similar ideas but using a video camera. What would be representative about school using this medium? The children could create a 60-second commercial for their school after studying commercials for other kinds of place. They might be given scope for either a 5-minute documentary about school life or perhaps the biography of a 'typical' pupil. They might create a 5-minute excerpt from a school soap opera. There is enough intensive work in any of these ideas to keep a class busy for weeks. They must constantly examine and read their own work in the light of their existing store of knowledge of the images produced previously by others.

I hope I have demonstrated that the attention and care given to print reading needs to be duplicated when media texts are the focus of attention. Children are learning to watch and listen all the time but the English teacher's intervention is as vital here as it is in the print reading process.

Reading the media – print texts

Part of the print reading process involves large sections of the media. Adolescents, especially boys, have a well-documented tendency to stop reading books, particularly fiction, from about the age of 12 onwards. However they are likely to continue reading comics, magazines and some newspapers.

I feel that work with newspapers is likely to be familiar enough to most English teachers and so will not labour the importance of such work. I have already made some points about the prejudices of some teachers (see Chapter 2). However, I think there is some danger that, when asked to write in newspaper form, pupils may simply yawn and say 'not again!' What we need, now that work with newspapers is relatively commonplace, is to make use of the spiral notion of media learning and to analyse how we can deepen and extend such learning. I discuss this in detail in Chapter 7.

There is a long history of classroom practice in which newspapers receive serious attention in English but magazines and comics have usually been excluded from consideration (see for example Murdock and Phelps 1973, Hoggart 1984). A critical moment comes for many teachers during silent reading lessons when pupils are allowed to select their own reading and a pupil wishes to read a magazine or comic, most English teachers refuse to allow such reading. There are many justifications given for such a refusal. If the pupil is interested enough then he/she will read such matter at home. Pupils should be reading real books in English. Reading magazines/comics is not serious reading and does not fit into an approved category. Parents and other staff would be shocked if they heard that pupils were reading comics in English.

The guilt that English teachers feel about such reading seems to me both unnecessary and misplaced. First if the point of the silent reading is to develop reading ability then the pupil's opportunity to read closely in a quiet atmosphere is the key element. Also if a pupil wishes to read the magazine but is told they must read a book instead then this seems to me to be just one more nail in the book-reading coffin for that individual. Any pupil can sit there and appear to read but real close reading comes from strong interest. When a class or group reads together then the context and pressure are quite different to a silent, individual reading.

More generally the important question seems to me to be whether the teacher would be intruding on pupils' entertainment by giving serious attention to the reading of comics and magazines. The research of Murdock and Phelps suggested that many working class pupils resented work like this because it did not fit in with their perception of what school was supposed to be about (Murdock and Phelps 1973: Part II). My view, based as much on my own teaching experience as any research evidence, is that pupils can be very interested in the close analysis of comics and magazines and that such work deepens understanding without damaging enjoyment. Most pupils do have a rather low opinion of such material however much they delight in reading it and they also feel rather confused about a teacher's motives in paying serious attention to it. The majority of such material is also very gender specific and so work with a mixed class may result initially in very banal responses at the level of 'that's just for girls'.

I would suggest the use of a deliberately distancing and challenging approach such as a whole class attempt to design a magazine that would appeal to both sexes or one aimed at a younger age group. A class might undertake:

- Very precise content analysis, documenting exactly what a popular magazine contains and in what proportions.
- A comparative study of several similar magazines to try and explain their different readerships.
- Surveys of readers in school and at the local bookshops.
- Selecting several stories at random and subjecting them to close analysis in terms of plot or agents.

In Chapter 6 I will provide a much fuller account of such work.

An aspect of reading that has steadily increased over the last decade has been the use of scripts. A number of publishers have provided examples of television plays for reading in school and it is no longer difficult to gain access to published film scripts. Some of these scripts are interesting for a group or a class to read aloud together. However, some are impossible to read like this and should not be approached in this way except to help pupils see that initially they hardly make sense. What I would argue is that these scripts are most useful as models for writing and this will be discussed in the next section.

A final point about reading is that pupils can learn a great deal from analysing the most ephemeral reading matter and putting their creative talents to work upon it. Their environment is full of printed T-shirts, posters, flyers, junk mail, packets, wrappers and so on. Each of these is a text and needs interpreting: one packet of cereal may have several hundred works printed on it, one piece of junk mail may contain an excellent example of a particular register of language. The key questions outlined in Chapter 4 can all be applied to such material with rich results. For example if a class examines cereal boxes to analyse the intended audience they may discover some interesting points about language; an older class might be able to make observations about the suggested life-styles and values implicit in the words and images. The move to imitative, parodying and original work is relatively easy after such close analysis.

Writing

As I have covered a range of points about media-related writing in the last section I intend in this section to concentrate on particular kinds of writing that might otherwise not appear in the English curriculum; Chapters 6 and 7 contain further suggestions and ideas.

For any English department a good principle to adopt is that every child should have the chance to write for an authentic audience in a variety of forms. It is valuable for a pupil to turn a short story into a radio play or the chapter of a fictional text into a camera script solely as an act of writing, but all writers benefit from following their work through to some form of production. A pupil can gain a whole new dimension of awareness by experiencing the process that takes an idea from its private, draft form into a final public production.

I discussed scripts above as more helpful for learning to write than to read. The writing of a script reveals just how much and how little most pupils know about the construction and origin of the words and movements that they regularly watch on screen. Many teachers are already encouraging their pupils to write scripts for drama and media work and so my concerns are with ways and means of building on such work.

English teachers are generally familiar with the idea of a storyboard. This is a series of images with a few key words accompanying each image which provide a primarily visual basis for a narrative or other kind of sequence; it gives a summary or short-hand version of the full narrative. A storyboard might arise from an existing script or might be the foundation on which the script is built. Like most apparently simply forms a storyboard is, in practice, a complex combination of words and images and pupils need to come to terms with this complexity without assuming too quickly that they can make much use of it.

Because of the complexities of storyboarding no class should rush into 'creative' work. Children can gain most by selecting from existing material using either a video extract which they break down into storyboard images or a short piece of script from which they design some key images. If the teacher combines both, i.e. use of a script and the video extract, then pupils gain some precise insight into the storyboard process and its relationship to the completed text. Moving from such analytical and interpretative work into producing a simple storyboard for a very brief sequence can build on these earlier ideas. Again it is often best to provide raw material in the form of an existing narrative or extract. In this way either an ordinary camera can be used producing a form of photo story or a video camera with all images pre-ordered so that editing will not be necessary. The teacher can add a great deal by taking a directorial job with each working group or class until pupils themselves wish to do so.

The principles underlying work with storyboards can be applied to other forms of media script. As mentioned above pupils find producing usable script challenging and difficult and so a department needs to take a developmental view of such work over a period of years. If pupils are already familiar with writing plays then this may provide some initial help. If pupils have some examples of script to look at and can relate them to a finished sequence this makes for an excellent starting point.

Writing a camera script is a very specialized task and can only be meaningful when a camera is eventually going to be used. Pupils can practise on existing material or write original pieces but they must have an opportunity to work with a camera. Learning about writing of this kind is often best achieved when a whole class works together, mapping out a narrative or documentary, designing particular sequences and then producing sections of script which eventually make up the whole text. Any experienced teacher will be able to tell from this simple description what a very demanding and complex operation this involves; however, I feel that it is infinitely preferable to single pupil authors always working on a script that will never be realized.

Radio programmes are a most underrated text in school and yet they offer great potential for intensive and productive work. One reason for radio's value is that in imitating radio programmes a reasonable quality of production can be achieved using an inexpensive tape recorder. It is far easier with a tape recorder to work anywhere, often well away from a noisy classroom. The medium of radio helps to focus the relationship between the written script and the spoken text; revisions and improvements are easier to identify and to carry out. Audiotape may seem far less powerful and stimulating than video but its importance lies in its particular intensity. Listening, as every teacher knows, is an especially demanding activity. The quality of writing is the crucial element and in this way radio offers a very interesting medium for pupils to work in.

One of the difficulties with all audio or video tape work is editing. There is no process more exacting and time consuming than editing and most schools are without sophisticated facilities to undertake such work. If the equipment is available then it offers great potential for pupils' learning but also significant problems of classroom management. In teaching the concept of editing it is much easier and more effective to set up tasks for pupils which give them written material which they have to edit from a particular point of view, letting them analyse and discuss differing results with others. Pupils using a word processor can edit script with ease and speed.

The original Cox Report placed Media Education and Information Technology (DES 1989: Chapter 9) somewhat cheek by jowl and gave the impression that they were rather like well-established neighbours. This juxtaposition elides all sorts of issues but there is no doubt that IT has brought many new facets to media education and there are two important areas to single out in relation to writing. I will premise these two points by stating, as above, that a word processor provides the best editing environment for any script or any piece of writing.

Desk Top Publishing (DTP) is an area in which concepts related to IT and media education come powerfully together. DTP provides scope in a number of ways for writing development but a most exciting aspect is the opportunity offered to organize images and text simultaneously. Such work is bound to be of interest to other departments in the secondary school but the English department can focus on developing pupils' understanding of text in relation to images. Work discussed earlier about anchoring an image can be very fully explored using DTP. A video camera can capture an image, such as the earlier example of the school, and the image can be digitized and made available as a still image in the DTP program's memory. The pupils might take photos and load them into the DTP program through a scanner. Once the images are there they can be adjusted in innumerable ways. It is the level of control over text and image that allows pupils to appreciate how closely they can orchestrate their finished piece for a particular audience or to fit in with a specific media context.

The other key area for media education is the use of software that helps to simulate specific media situations. There are a number of programs which place pupils in the role of newsgatherers and editors, the news arrives at regular intervals and the pupils have a task to accomplish in a given time. Other programs create more dramatic scenarios in which some pupils will be in role and deciding what information they should or should not release to the public through the media. Such work creates excellent opportunities for all kinds of reflection on how the media operates and controls information and on what it is like to be working within the media and subject to its constraints and pressures. All four language modes are in operation here but the writing process is intensely illuminated for pupils as they try to capture the flow of information, constantly revising and adjusting their copy.

Speaking and listening

The 1980s might be characterized in English teaching as the decade when the importance of speaking and listening finally gained real acceptance. This change is most evident in the formal realm of HMI documents, the GCSE criteria and syllabuses and now in the National Curriculum itself. This development has profound implications of its own but it has certainly opened the way to very important work in media education.

It is worth reflecting here on one simple but vital point. The world of literature for many children is only available in the world of school; the world of the media is available and encompassing for all children, regardless of class, gender or race. I am not suggesting that these latter differences are unimportant in relation to media education but I am suggesting that the media have a kind of universality that can bring people into a useful, interpretive community. One thing that all adults recognize about themselves and children is that the media are a constant topic of conversation. Very often such talk is about the content of a programme or a news item but equally it may be about preference and value. There has always been a line of argument that this universality is exactly what makes the media so influential and noxious, the teacher's job, following this view, must be to shut the media out.

What I would suggest is that the media are a very powerful stimulus to speaking and listening and that the bridge, for example, from social chat to formal discussion can be readily made. In this sense the media provide a constant flow of topics and ideas that can be used judiciously by the teacher; this is hardly a new idea. However, I would argue that the teacher's real job is not just to take advantage of this incidental flow of opportunities but to bring the children's intellectual faculties to bear on to both the content and also, vitally, on to the media themselves. There is always a danger that the vague, window on the world view of the media may prevail if the media's content is seen as unproblematic. I think that whatever age the class a teacher can explore at appropriate times not just 'Did you see that programme last night?' but the context of the programme and the structure of its making. Such work can latch on to the spontaneous interest generated by any particular media item but bring with it a systematic and developmental methodology.

For the English teacher there is no doubt that one of the richest sources of spoken language is the media; radio, television and film provide us with a constant flow of spoken language and an archive of language in the process of change. Almost all, perhaps all, aspects of Knowledge About Language might be covered through media-based work. Therefore in helping pupils to understand how speaking and listening operate, the media provide a constant source of material for pupils to analyse and reflect upon. The most striking aspects of spoken language that the media provide access to are accent, register, voice, tone, vocabulary and contextual appropriateness.

However, every speaking situation has a context and the situations within the media are very particular indeed. Pupils can learn very rapidly from breaking down the apparent naturalness of a chat show or *Any Questions* not only about people's speaking and listening but just as much about the construction of such programmes. Who are the speakers talking to? Is their language 'natural'? What language does a host use and how does it affect the guest? Can we compare such a situation to one that pupils may face, a discussion at an interview for example?

The last question immediately highlights the interrelationship between such analysis and practical work. However much we live in an age of technology, children are still relatively unfamiliar with themselves on video and on audio-tape. Almost all children are comfortable with photographs because they tend to have grown up with them and think of them as normal, everyday artefacts. The issue for English teachers is twofold. First there is a whole dimension of self-awareness that can be explored through capturing someone on tape. To a large extent such work is only incidentally related to understanding about the media. It is highly charged and challenging work and children feel very vulnerable to their peers once they have committed themselves on to tape. However, tape allows them to explore their own accents, mannerisms, image and so on in a way that can sharply enhance their understandings of speaking and listening.

The second point is that this whole dimension of self-consciousness is an inevitable and potentially valuable part of practical media sessions but, as with similar work in drama, it can be an obstacle that must be overcome. In order to produce interesting media material of their own pupils need a chance to move on from the self-conscious stage to a consciousness of situation and context. For example, once a few pupils have tried to read the news to a video camera, have watched themselves on tape and compared their efforts with those of professional newscasters they recognize that the professionals must be having some additional help somewhere. Once the idea of an autocue is understood then it becomes much more possible to analyse and reflect on the particular speech style of news and its presumed audience. Pupils can then imitate and parody this style and discuss with much less self-consciousness the role of a newscaster and their own attempts to emulate such a role. In order to understand about the reading of the news pupils are simultaneously exploring media concepts and concepts about spoken language.

The same is true of self-consciousness in radio work. Pupils have to overcome the embarrassment at the sounds of their own voices through focusing on a context. How do we know who is talking on the radio whether in a live interview or a scripted play? To find the answer pupils have to listen intently and analyse their findings. They can then move to practical work with an understanding of a contextualized model as a basis. Radio also offers unlimited possibilities for imaginative work that television and film can never do because it removes the insistence of sight, pupils can escape from the constant nagging demands of being 'realistic'. The voice, sound effects, silence, these elements can combine to offer the opportunity for pupils with limited equipment to create rich, aural patterns.

Media and knowledge about language

One reason why media education received relatively little attention during the construction of National Curriculum English was that the Knowledge About Language components of the subject dominated both the Cox committee's and then teachers' concerns. The LINC Reader produced to support the LINC project (Carter 1991) contains barely a reference to media education. This is especially ironic as the kind of systematic attention to language proposed for pupils in Key Stages 3 and 4 fits very well with work on a number of media education concepts. I have discussed earlier (Chapter 4) how important it is for pupils to recognize that, as well as using language in its conventional sense, the media have their own language.

The main point to develop here is related to knowledge and understanding about language. The English teacher is faced with the challenge of developing pupils' understanding about language without obfuscating the process with a dogmatic approach to terminology. I believe that pupils need some understanding of large concepts before they can appreciate specific points of detail of the language system.

If we take a concept like language variety, for example the way language users adapt their usage for the current situation, then media texts provide some of the most valuable material, whether audio-visual or print, for such work. If we take a relationship like language and power then it is relatively easy to find examples of media texts where the relationship of language to power is clearly exposed. The television or radio interview is frequently an example of dominance at a number of levels, from the personal to the ideological. In writing, newspapers constantly provide evidence of the insidious nature of discrimination both racial and sexual. In order to develop linguistic understanding pupils need to develop media understanding, the two are complementary and interlinked.

Many teachers already use media material for these purposes but what KAL should bring is attention to language detail within larger issues and concepts. To appreciate the rhetoric of a newspaper editorial or to penetrate the supposed neutrality of certain kinds of reporting pupils need to explain how they recognize that is happening. In some instances this will mean using linguistic and media-related terminology in order to be precise and the teacher can introduce and teach these terms through media work. Pupils can also learn to articulate their understanding of complex issues such as language and power through carrying out practical work. After the practical work is completed pupils can then reflect on and analyse the complex issues from their own recently increased awareness. Chapters 6 and 7 examine a number of further issues about the value of practical work.

Media education and cross-curricular issues

Media education has received relatively little attention in National Curriculum documents other than English. However, all subject teachers have to consider the place of the five cross-curricular themes (Environmental Education, Citizenship, Health, Personal and Social Education, and Economic and Industrial Understanding) in their work and these themes provide excellent opportunities for media work to spread across the whole curriculum. The role of the media in all these areas is extremely powerful and so departments may be able to collaborate in a number of ways simultaneously using the themes and media work.

One pressing concern in relation to cross-curricular themes is the existing overcrowding in the English curriculum. How can English accommodate even more demands on its already over-stretched time? The only realistic way is through approaching topics that allow for a number of areas of English and other important areas like the themes to be covered at once. The themes themselves have always played a part in English as is revealed by any analysis of pre-National Curriculum English curricula.

I will use just two examples to illustrate how a department can develop media education and make a positive contribution to the cross-curricular themes. Economic and Industrial Understanding is a theme that some English teachers find hard to see a place for in their teaching; in my own research I find that at least 80 per cent of English teachers put this theme last of the five, both in terms of their personal interest and its importance to English teaching. Work on the media provides some excellent and extremely relevant ways of engaging with the theme. A familiar topic like advertising offers very good scope. Instead of simply asking pupils to analyse and/or create advertisements they can be given the role of an agency with a limited budget and with important decisions to make about running a campaign. If a class are working on a magazine they can decide to publish it, finding out costs, choosing a suitable print run and seeking advertising and other kinds of support. They can even investigate different economic models, choosing to act as a cooperative – i.e. profits and losses equally shared – or a capitalist model with owners of the means of production and/or the backers taking most of the profit.

Another example concerns the idea of institutions. The concept of a media institution is difficult to get across and pupils generally find the idea of ownership rather abstract not to say uninteresting. However some under-standing of media institutions has a crucial part to play in their general appreciation of how the media operate. I interpret Economic and Industrial Understanding as a theme designed to provoke questions and concerns. Using this interpretation pupils can investigate a number of facets of media ownership. The ownership and control of newspapers can be a good starting point and some pupils will already have some knowledge of media barons like Maxwell and Murdoch. A useful beginning can be made by pupils exploring the roles of editor and owner deciding over a scoop, revelations about the royal family are always good material; the scoop will boost cir-culation but it may damage the owner's chance of a knighthood, what will the paper do? Eventually pupils can move on to considering how certain organizations can control large sections of the media across the world. For example after discussing their views on satellite television pupils could be asked to consider what would make a successful satellite station aimed at their age group; who would be interested in owning access like this to young people and what might be the motivation?

Another theme that might be explored is Environmental Education. Envi-ronmental topics may at first seem better suited to Geography or Science but in fact they have great potential for English amd media work. For example, a class might take on and develop a drama about the building of a new motorway or the siting of a new factory close to an existing community which is divided in its reaction to the development. A fundamental part of such a drama would be the role of the media. At first local radio and tele-vision would be involved then perhaps national interest would develop with politicians entering the debate. Pupils in role as local residents can develop campaigns to promote their views. A teacher may introduce ideas of media ownership too: what happens if the local paper is owned by a property devel-oper who stands to gain from the new development?

Conclusion

I hope this chapter has illustrated how the traditional concerns of English and some of the new demands of the National Curriculum can be successfully covered by media education work. The next two chapters go into more depth, examining detailed schemes of work for media education in English.

6 Facing issues and overcoming anxieties

In this chapter – and the subsequent one – I hope to illustrate that media education is pushing at and reshaping English and is also offering ways of working that are challenging, liberating and that constitute excellent practice. This chapter attempts to remove some persistent and damaging obstacles to such good practice and includes a number of examples of teaching strategies and ideas. Chapter 7 is wholly concerned with more fully documented examples of schemes of work.

As a preliminary, however, I need to consider a general point about English teachers before moving to the first specific issue. The teacher of English has acquired over the century almost equal weights of responsibility and scorn. Teachers of English have claimed so much for their subject, moral uplift, spiritual and personal growth, understanding of the greatest literature, etc. that it is no wonder that their mission often seems impossible (see Chapter 1). Margaret Mathieson's important study of English teachers (Mathieson 1975), also discussed in Chapter 2, concludes with two chapters emphasizing how difficult the role of the classroom English teacher has become; her chapters are entitled 'The English Teacher's Role: Strain and Conflict' and 'Interest and Enjoyment: Teachers and Pupils'. Taken overall the study is conservative and cautious in its conclusions yet its analysis is very relevant for the 1990s. Her main thrust is that 'romantic radicalism' and 'romantic progressivism' put extraordinary pressures on the English teacher. These 'romantic' approaches to teaching demand a highly personal, child-centred classroom style involving constant discussion of relevant and controversial material. Mathieson argues that the effect of these demands on the English teacher is an erosion of confidence in the study of literature and language. She goes on to state (1975: 224):

> In their early days of responsibility for forming the characters of all their pupils, English teachers were asked to be inspiring – to negotiate as ambassadors of culture, to fight like warriors against commercial forces. Since then

they have been told constantly that their sensitive and sympathetic guidance is indispensable in promoting their pupils' growth – but that they must withdraw, be inconspicuous. Today they are asked – by the radicals – as are all teachers – to stop being teachers altogether.

She argues that an impossible tension is created for most English teachers, they are thrown back almost completely on the resources of personality and yet at the same time they are expected to avoid dominating the classroom. This is an over-simplification but still a useful one, it can help us to reconsider and perhaps reformulate the English teacher's role. I shall develop this point more fully below.

At the same time as English teachers have been claiming the moral and aesthetic high ground, employers and politicians berate them for school leavers' inability, as they see it, to read, write, understand grammar, speak properly and, most grievous of all, spell. Barely a week goes by without someone who proudly parades as a virtue his (I use the gender advisedly) complete lack of expertise but claims to have sound, common sense and demands to know why English teachers no longer teach the basics, etc., etc. Mathieson's views are nothing like these but the latter views are, of course, far more powerful in the public domain. As a direct result of politicians believing that they know more about the place of language study in teaching English than English teachers themselves the Language in the National Curriculum project had its materials brutally and abruptly censored (see *The Times Educational Supplement*, any issue during June and July 1991).

I hope this backward glance makes clear the need to devote a chapter to issues and anxieties. Media education may be seen by many teachers as threatening what little stability they have left. My rationale has been to select a small number of key issues and to devote some space to each in the hope that such close attention will firmly establish a basis for more positive and optimistic attitudes to prevail.

Popular fiction

If the success of English teaching was to be measured by the proportion of the adult population who regularly or occasionally read works from the literary canon, the Great Tradition, then it might seem that the whole endeavour has failed dismally. If the expectations were lowered somewhat and the measure of success was the extent to which pupils had enjoyed and valued great works of literature during their school days things would still look pretty bad. Paradoxically if the measure was the proportion of the adult population who enjoy and valued 'popular fiction' then suddenly English teaching would appear to be very successful indeed. This hypothesis contains within it, I suggest, a very serious point. English teachers are expected to condemn and dismiss popular fiction and to encourage their pupils to write as if it did not exist. The models of good writing offered to pupils in some schools are exclusively the 'great' writers or, and this is perhaps even more demanding, children are abjured to find an original voice of their own. These models and such demands are excellent as far as they go but they only cover some aspects of literature.

As Gemma Moss expresses it in *Un/popular Fictions* (Moss 1989: 103):

> . . . teachers use the word 'derivative' to dismiss writing they do not like and cannot approve of, whether from a Leavisite, Media Studies or anti-sexist perspective. The word is used selectively in relation to a particular body of texts: broadly, those which reproduce the central features of popular fiction. Inevitably, its use is therefore bound up with particular systems of values, whether moral, aesthetic or political. Moreover, teachers working within a Leavisite, Media Studies or anti-sexist perspective are concerned that in reproducing a form of which they disapprove children are also endorsing a set of values which teachers don't like. This turns the writers of such fictions into at best hapless victims of a powerful ideology they cannot contest, or at worst co-conspirators with a set of values which works against their own long-term interests.

One of her main arguments is that such teacherly judgements of 'derivative' work are not only wrong but that they are missing the main point. Moss recognizes that there is a stock response to popular fiction every bit as clichéd as the form it derides for being cliché-ridden, she summarizes it as follows (1989: 39):

> Popular fiction provides ready-made and easy answers to the complex problems with which children could creatively wrestle as they write . . . Firmly wedded to the notion that to read is to experience, the teacher's task is to provide the best sort of experience through offering 'good' literature. [Teachers should] . . . send pupils out into the world enriched by a knowledge of great art, inoculated against the corrupting influence of mass culture.

Her answer to this traditional dismissal of popular fiction is to explore closely how adolescents play with and interrogate such texts in their reading and especially in their writing. Adolescents do like the usually clear and narrow structure of certain genres like the romantic or the thriller story, the pleasure of these texts is often in their certainties and slight but occasional twists: they are, in Barthes's term, very readerly (Barthes 1974). However, the pupils *also* explore, develop and often oppose any simple reading of these popular forms. Through close analysis of a number of girls' and boys' stories she shows how much more complex and developmental such stories can be than a cursory and dismissive reading would allow (see especially Moss 1989: Chapters 4 and 5).

I am arguing, in support of Moss, that English teachers should seize upon popular fiction with genuine enthusiasm, not evangelical desires for reform. It seems to me that if some of the approaches more characteristic of recent literary criticism and of media are brought into the classroom in a suitable

form for adolescents then the place of popular fiction becomes easy to identify and put into productive use. Instead of being a threatening and dangerous presence it becomes part of the spectrum of reading that is open for
enjoyment, analysis and criticism.

It would be helpful if we knew when popular fiction enters the consciousness. Is there such a thing for 10 year olds, do they have views on
serious as opposed to entertaining reading? I feel sure, at least, that they
have some ideas and opinions worth taking account of. Adults themselves
start being anxious once their children become genuinely independent
readers, from about the age of 8 onwards. For the adults the enemies seem
to be *those* writers who are thoroughly enjoyed by all sorts of children.
I imagine that a few years ago Enid Blyton would have been the main
contender. Perhaps Roald Dahl has now replaced her? Incidentally, some
ongoing research of my own into formative reading experiences suggests that
at least 80 per cent of English teachers under 35 went through a serious
Blyton reading phase some time between the ages of 7 and 12 and all
survived; the great majority are women and, despite the way Blyton depicts
girls, they know a sexist writer when they read one. Returning to adult,
especially parental anxieties, it is inevitable that teachers themselves are
nervous about paying serious attention to books that are popular but that
lack the stamp of critical approval. Pupils, gradually recognize that what they
like reading may not be a suitable topic for conversation in front of their
teacher. I would suggest that many aspects of popular fiction are not only
worth analysing and reflecting on with children but that they can enjoy such
work without feeling as if some 'Big Brother' is checking on their reading
habits.

For example children at Key Stage 3 are perfectly able to work on some
important concepts in relation to popular fiction. The first concept is popularity itself. It is easy to get hold of bestseller lists for all categories of fiction
including children's and to set the class the task of investigating the validity
of such lists. Pupils can analyse the reading interests of their own class and
compare it with others. If they are expected to keep reading records and
journals then pupils can have a look at the way interests have changed. They
can look for the influence of television adaptations or films based on books.
Equally children can be asking family members what they read when they
were young and what they read now, documenting this as evidence. It does
not seem intrusive or middle class to me to ask all children to undertake such
work even if their family provides no evidence of reading. There may be
opportunities in such pupil research to help all pupils understand some of
the broader issues related to literacy.

All this work is background research but provides a wealth of information
for everyone, not least the teacher. Pupils can then move to the study of
some popular authors and popular forms. It does not detract from their
enjoyment to analyse the basic components of a Blyton or a Dahl story;

pupils may have a wealth of knowledge to draw on and can look at plot structures, types of character, gender roles, beginnings and endings, particular uses of language. Instead of simply designing yet another book cover, pupils can study how a popular author is marketed and promoted. If some 'new' Blyton stories were discovered how would they be marketed and sold to contemporary readers?

After intensive work of the above kind pupils can be given the highly demanding task of imitating a popular author using a popular form. This work will need more conscious attention than producing an original piece. If pupils work in pairs or groups then they can help each other with revisions and redraftings until all are agreed that the imitation has succeeded. The teacher can introduce the term 'popular classics' and ask pupils to look at extracts from a whole variety of authors and to consider, dispassionately, what must have made them popular once and why they may appeal to some readers now. There is plenty of scope here for work by younger secondary pupils on pre-twentieth century literature such as *A Christmas Carol*, *Black Beauty*, *Treasure Island*, *The Water Babies* and other texts from the canon of children's literature.

Many pupils working in Key Stage 4 (if present arrangements continue) will have the opportunity for wider reading which provides a perfect format for work with popular fiction, I will discuss this opportunity in Chapter 7. However, even now a substantial number of pupils are entered either for English only or not at all. If English teachers are to live up to the intention of helping school leavers to be comprehensively literate and also to become readers who actively enjoy reading, then I would argue that work with popular fiction is essential to fulfil that intention. To extend my argument, what is the point of presenting literature as though it were a fixed and dead system with its value hierarchies firmly established, when there is no such fixed hierarchy? If we wish children to take adult reading seriously then I would argue that they must comprehend what that activity is about and also be allowed to discuss what they know about it.

I would suggest that a media education perspective on popular fiction involves helping pupils to look at all of the key areas of understanding (agencies, categories, technologies, languages, audiences and representations). Such understandings might be encouraged in a number of ways especially if younger pupils have already carried out some of the suggestions above about Key Stage Three. I shall devote part of Chapter 7 to two examples of teaching popular fiction at GCSE level, one as part of English, one in relation to wider reading.

To sum up, the study and enjoyment of popular fiction will not and should not replace what might, to echo Gemma Moss's title, be termed the study of unpopular fiction. Pupils can and should engage with the whole range of adult reading. They can appreciate differences between how one book, perhaps a thriller by Jack Higgins, is produced and sold and how

Great Expectations is marketed. They can also compare what it is like to read these books and where the differences and similarities in that experience may come from. English teachers, if they are feeling defensive or insecure about work on popular fiction, can tell parents and governors that such knowledge is vital in producing literate, sensitive adult readers who understand how books are produced and why they remain one of our chief forms of pleasure and most fundamental sources of understanding.

Adaptations

Once upon a time adaptations were simple. There was book or a play and then someone made a version of it for radio, television or film. Now this process can happen in any order. The Turtle craze (*circa* 1989–91?), spawned from comic book characters, led to a television series, story books, video tapes, taped stories, films using 'real' people, a proliferation of spin-offs of all kinds. This example is not a simple adaptation but it illustrates the complexity of processes that may extend the life of some very basic narrative elements. The film of *The French Lieutenant's Woman* was in one sense a straightforward adaptation of Fowles's novel, and, in my opinion, a very successful one because the screenplay writer, Harold Pinter, used an inventive idea to give the film a truer resemblance to reader's experience of the two endings in the original novel.

The adaptation is one of the most fascinating aspects of a multimedia society. The English teacher is usually concerned with the film of the book or the film of the play, very often Shakespeare. From my observations of teachers and student teachers, current practice with adaptations could be divided into the following categories:

1 *Now watch the film but do not mix it up with the original* – This approach mainly operates the audio-visual text as a reward for slogging through the original, and follow up work might involve some discussion of differences between the 'versions'.
2 *What has happened to the original?* – In this approach the two texts are studied in parallel with reading of the audio-visual text sometimes preceding the written, follow up work will involve close comparisons of some 'scenes' and pupils will have opportunities for creative and analytical work on either text. There will almost always be some sense that the original is the more valued text.
3 *Texts and contexts* – This approach uses similar pedagogical strategies to (2) but with a different aim and without emphasizing or necessarily privileging one of the texts.

One of the chief differences between (3) and (2) is that the former examines who made both texts and considers media questions like agencies and audiences. For example Spielberg's treatment of *The Color Purple* can only be understood in relation to Hollywood and the financial machinations of the American film industry.

Category (3) is the one that English departments should adopt for at least some texts. There may be numerous other occasions when classes read an audio-visual text for quite different purposes but there should be occasions for them to develop an understanding of the processes and purposes of adaptations. In order to use (3) teachers have to surrender the validity of the original and allow pupils to examine both texts and their contexts. Over the years I have seen very rewarding work with trios of fairly standard secondary texts such as the novel, play and film texts of *An Inspector Calls, Billy Liar, Gregory's Girl*, and *Kes*. Pupils have to work very hard and need a great deal of help from the teacher to grasp the various relationships between such trios but the result can be an understanding of the way each medium both constrains and extends the basic narrative.

I think that English teachers should stop feeling guilty about the concept they have of using adaptations as a kind of reward, justified on the grounds that the important original is good literature and so it is reasonable to watch the film. The important point is that children need to understand that texts, i.e. basic narratives are infinitely adaptable but that every such adaptation is also a transformation because of the medium and the historical context. Showing an 'old' adaptation of a text can help pupils to understand how social forces are at work in shaping that particular production and how current audiences might reject its standpoint. It has become an increasingly standard activity in English to ask pupils to adapt texts from one medium to another. Their understanding of the process can be enhanced by the study of the process itself just as their practical awareness can inform their analysis of professionally produced texts.

There are of course many adaptations of texts from the literary canon and these give no qualms to A-Level and GCSE teachers. As a final point I would like to suggest that pupils' and students' understanding of publishing and other forms of media production can be enhanced by some analysis and reflection on what happens to the books that undergo this new canonization, for example becoming a classic serial or a film by Merchant and Ivory. Questions like 'What happens to the book's sales?', 'How is the book marketed in relation to the audio-visual text?', 'What audience do the producers have in mind for each of the texts?', 'Who reads such books as a result of the adaptation?' can provoke some serious and close analysis of media institutions and some interesting reflections on literature.

Shakespeare

The teaching of Shakespeare in schools is a remarkable phenomenon; Shakespeare is an institution, an industry, the ultimate symbol of culture. No English teacher can approach the teaching of a Shakespeare text without dealing with some of this historical baggage. Shakespeare also occupies an extraordinary position in media terms. Not only have there been many film, radio and television adaptations but Shakespeare continues to be news; as an icon of culture and of Englishness no media reference to him or his work can be without some positioning by the commentator, some attempt to place the audience.

As regards the nature of teaching about Shakespeare, until the development of active approaches to the text the majority of pupils who read some Shakespeare unquestionably left school with knowledge of a text but without much appreciation or understanding of Shakespeare as a dramatist. One, highly productive, and by no means new, approach to Shakespeare's work, is through drama, treating the play as it actually is, a working script. I am entirely in support of such an approach and work on adaptations of Shakespeare is not a substitute for it. Work on adaptations of Shakespeare is one important way of approaching the plays themselves and it is also a very successful way of integrating media education with traditionally literary English work. The Cox Report fully endorses the active approach to Shakespeare and then suggests that another valuable way to approach the plays is through the 'use of film and video recordings' (DES 1989: 7.16). All pupils are expected to have access to Shakespeare but not necessarily through a straight reading of a play.

There are dozens of examples of adaptations of Shakespeare and so I will concentrate on just six. I should first restate the chief point from the previous section, that the study of an adaptation cannot be viewed only as a way of reflecting on the original, it must involve reflection on the medium of adaptation. I feel it is especially important to stress this because Shakespeare bears so much cultural weight that teachers and pupils are easily bowed down by it.

Many pupils certainly approach Shakespeare more apprehensively than they do a visit to the dentist and it is worth considering briefly what can be done about this fearful, negative attitude. My own view is that at a deep level many self-proclaimed 'lovers' of Shakespeare do not want the majority of the population to enjoy his plays; their real motive is to make him 'caviare to the general'. Therefore the image projected of his work is that of a museum to which very few, privileged people have tickets. I should like to suggest that the deconstruction of this image is vital, it is, in a very real sense, an essential aspect of media education. My own work with pupils on Shakespeare always began with a deliberate shock tactic, looking at how coarse some of his jokes are or simulating an Elizabethan audience to show how he had to seize the audience's attention. To those who see such devices as gimmicky I would simply suggest that they employ the same distancing and making strange techniques that I advocate throughout the book. Pupils never need to be told that Shakespeare is important or highly valued, they know that without any empathetic feeling for the idea. This notion is very comfortable and easy and allows them to position Shakespeare as 'other'. What they need to know is that Shakespeare always was, and is, popular and was astonishingly good at providing entertainment; such a concept is a necessary shock to children and takes away their comfortable preconceptions.

This point about deconstructing the élitists' image of Shakespeare is essential for any work on adaptations of his plays. If some attempt is not made at it then pupils are likely to approach a film or television production with all the stock responses that society has encouraged them to have. Adaptations themselves may provide material for such deconstruction or they may, like the BBC Shakespeares, collude with and reinforce the idea of there being only a small, privileged audience that can 'appreciate' his work.

Zeffirelli's *Romeo and Juliet* is one of the film adaptations of Shakespeare most used in secondary schools and it contains a whole range of possibilities. Those who watch for category (1) (see above) may at least notice that the film changes a few things. Those who watch for category (2) can develop an awareness of the simplifications and streamlinings of the plot that allow for visual richness such as the incident where the Friar's inspiration about how to help the lovers comes from his glance at the cross in his church, an image which the audience sees in a close-up. Those using category (3) might not only develop these understandings but also go further. Shakespeare used contemporary dress and little scenery; how much meaning in the film depends on the elaborate costuming and 'authentic', medieval backdrop? What impact is made by the semi-nudity of the bedroom scene? Compare this discrete use of sexual reference with the comparative bowdlerizing of the play's language. What can we learn about the contemporary audiences for each of the texts from a study of both?

Olivier's Second World War film of *Henry V* can only be understood as a production aimed at a particular audience at a particular time. Its emphatic appeals to patriotism and Henry's right to win reveal not only the director's intentions but also the ideology of the time. Branagh's recent film provides an ideal counterpoint, it is altogether more sombre, more cynical and again revealing about how viewpoints have changed. With these films pupils might gain some awareness of the appropriation of Shakespeare to something very local indeed; instead of being a 'universal' and 'for all time', suddenly he seems fitted into a narrow, English piece of propaganda.

There are a number of versions of *Macbeth*, notably a BBC production, Polanski's film and a version made for schools of the Ian McKellen and Judi Dench stage production; no doubt there are others. These are radically different productions in innumerable ways. The use of excerpts from these texts can first help pupils to understand how the printed marks on the page can be so variously interpreted and translated into an audio–visual spectacle. They can also illustrate how the constraints and opportunities of each medium affect the meaning of the play.

Finally Shakespeare is not perceived as just a writer of plays. However much I attempted to break down my pupils' prejudices about Shakespeare those prejudices are everywhere and constantly reinforced. It is always difficult to help pupils or even A-Level students to grasp concepts like that of a cultural institution but considering Shakespeare as an institution can be relatively straightforward. If instead of asking a set of questions about literary merit one takes a different approach some interesting considerations emerge. For example 'What is the Shakespeare industry worth to our economy?', 'How many people work in the Shakespeare industry?', 'What does it cost to see a Shakespeare play?', 'What kind of audience goes to see Shakespeare?', 'How many pupils/parents have seen a Shakespeare play for their own pleasure?', 'How many parents support the subsidizing of theatres, like the RSC?' I cannot see how anyone can object to such questions being asked and, possibly, answered. First, from a literary point of view, such questions cannot be separated from Shakespeare's importance as a writer. Second the cross-curricular themes of the National Curriculum such as Economic and Industrial Understanding and Citizenship are being effectively covered. Third, those critics of teachers who constantly deride trendiness and subversiveness in the classroom can surely see how such work explores the traditional influence and power of the cultural establishment.

Soap opera

There can be few forms of entertainment that attract both viewers and scornful comments in such massive numbers as soap operas. The current favourite soap opera, whichever one it happens to be, will usually top the viewing figures for all programmes every week and there will also be several additional 'soaps' within the top ten, most watched, programmes. For many parents and authority figures, especially politicians, soap opera epitomizes everything that they fear about television's power to 'hypnotize' viewers, particularly young viewers. Soap opera, however, appears to be one of the few types of programme that attracts a genuinely wide spectrum of viewers across class, gender, race and age. As far as I know some teachers watch them too but I am not aware of any research which might tell us if there are significant numbers of teacher soap watchers.

I do not plan here to give much background to individual soap operas or to add to the more public debate about them. There are useful books and articles that cover these areas (see for example Buckingham 1987a, b). My intention is to put forward some reasons why an English teacher might devote some precious time to working on them and to provide a few suggestions about how such work might be undertaken. I am concerned, as with previous sections in this chapter, to remove the anxiety that many teachers may feel about the 'worth' of soap opera. I suspect that many educators, even those who personally enjoy this form of entertainment, worry about its low status in the conventional cultural hierarchy.

It is worth pausing for a moment to question the nature of soap opera. There is unquestionably a soap opera form, but it is not uniform, even though it has powerful conventions and, by now, traditions. There is a considerable range in location and in the social and economic status of the main characters. The most effective way to define the soap seems to be that it aims to provide a continuous and continuing narrative based around a specific location with regular characters who are more or less constant in their importance; within this overarching narrative there will always be several story strands woven together. One of the more bizarre results of such a form is that the actors and actresses may die but the part goes on: in the long-running radio soap, *The Archers*, this even leads to what might be called the Dorian Gray syndrome where characters age more slowly than in real time. The definition above does not include some of the characteristics of the form such as the use of coincidence, the discovery of long-lost characters and so on, all of which connect it very powerfully with traditional, 'serious' literature.

The narrative elements in soap opera embrace everything from the humble and mundane to the most intensely dramatic events in human experience. What actually seems to upset opponents and critics of the genre is that 'ordinary' people, including large numbers of children, like it and find it satisfying. I suggest that English teachers need to take their responsibilities about narrative very seriously, and this does not mean always being formal and lugubrious about soap opera itself. This responsibility involves an openness about narrative, a willingness to be investigative and collaborative with pupils in trying to understand what makes certain narrative forms so powerful.

On the basis of such an investigative approach a fundamental reason for undertaking work on soap opera should come from a teacher's individual need to test a hypothesis. Perhaps the teacher believes that pupils are slavishly and passively following banal storylines, simultaneously swallowing whatever values happen to be embedded in the narrative? On the other hand the teacher may expect pupils to be highly knowledgeable and critically detached, able to enjoy but also parody and deride this particular television form. In either case it is quite likely that many pupils have closer knowledge of soap opera than the teacher and far more awareness of the media – especially press – coverage that is always attendant on the programmes and the current actors and actresses. Certainly, in my own experience, this was always true, though it is worth stressing here that many teenagers aged 14 and above do not devote much of their time to following any particular soap. So the teacher needs to adopt a genuinely open and investigative approach but without relinquishing the necessary analytical rigour that the use of the key media questions will bring.

Another powerful reason for investigating soap opera is for the insights it offers into narrative. There is narrative at the fundamental and universal level in soap opera, what is it that appeals to so many viewers? What is the structure of narrative in soap opera? Is it the same in several soaps and does the same structure exist in other kinds of text? How much do different pupils know about the construction of the various story threads and topical issues that are generally woven into the programme's typical tapestry?

In order to answer these questions a variety of analytic tasks can be deployed. Pupils can create maps to show basic settings, charts to show character attributes and public and private relationships. They can use story-lines to show the various threads becoming more or less prominent. They can analyse episodes to reveal their literally episodic structure, the rise and fall of dramatic tension as the programme moves to its conventionally climactic, regular cliff hanger. They can identify similar characters in differ-ent soaps and examine their roles in relation to other characters. They can identify and analyse the gender roles in one or more soap operas and reflect on the power or lack of it exercised by the sexes. They can use drama to role play seriously, or in parody, the dialogue from typical scenes, examining to what extent it follows natural speech.

A scheme of work that allows pupils to compare a number of series brings with it opportunities to investigate all the above and to pay more attention to concepts of audience. Pupils can analyse how soap operas might be dif-ferentiated by their attention to status, e.g. compare and contrast *Dynasty* and *Coronation Street*. They can examine transmission times and reflect on the appeal of various soaps as defined by who might be able to view them live.

If teachers want to try out practical work then I would suggest that there is plenty of interesting drama work to be done without using a camera. Pupils can write scripts and try acting out scenes, they can improvise based on structured scenarios, they can parody the typical compressing of events through farce and so on. However if a teacher wants to explore the pro-duction process in more depth then the use of radio soap opera as the model can be very productive. *The Archers*, Radio Four's saga of country life, is listened to by many teachers but that is not my reason for putting it forward. Television soap opera is comfortable and familiar to pupils, radio soap is relatively strange and unknown.

Listening to *The Archers* allows pupils to discover its language and con-ventions, its episodic structures and narrative devices. Analysis of episodes can lead pupils into writing and producing imitative material on tape. An especially challenging possibility involves the design of a pilot programme for a new radio soap with pupils considering the likely audience and writing promotional material to persuade programme controllers to give them a chance to try it out. This approach can be used on a pilot television series equally effectively but any practical work may be more successful if it does not involve the use of video. Even though many soap operas are notoriously low-budget productions there is little point in pupils attempting to emulate how they look unless their intention is to parody. If parody is the aim then poor camera work and glimpses of odd apparently unrelated people can only add to the comedy.

This latter point about the low budget of many soap operas can provide another productive approach to studying this form, particularly for older pupils. Some soap operas, especially American ones, are clearly expensive productions and they rely heavily on established television and film stars and cameo appearances by other stars. Others, often British or Australian, have a much more modest, deliberately unglamorous look. Considered from this point of view pupils can examine both what lies behind such differences and also explore in some depth the kind of audience that the programmes are trying to attract. What kinds of viewer loyalty are created by these different programmes and are they sustained? Pupils can investigate the loyalties of older members of their family and of their local community. Such work can be much enhanced by studying the advertising placed before, during and after the programme and through analysing the writing about the programmes in magazines and newspapers.

In conclusion, work on soap opera can be just as complex and demanding for pupils as any other form of narrative analysis. I suggest that English teachers have much to gain from such work and a great deal to learn themselves. Through such attention they put themselves in touch with one of the greatest currents of narrative interest in contemporary life. Any teacher who worries about their ignorance of the day-to-day content of soap opera can put such concerns aside and try to develop an approach that allows all pupils, whether soap-opera fans or not, to analyse and reflect on the narrative energy and power of the form; I hope the brief suggestions above provide some potential ways into close study of the form. In my experience the teacher can be a genuinely neutral and disinterested moderator of this work, which is rarely the case with print texts. The teacher also needs to exercise considerable control and intellectual discipline with classes to help them avoid trivial comparisons between various programmes. In other words work on soap opera is the exact opposite to a soft option and needs to be approached with an awareness by the teacher of its very real demands.

Pupils as audience

On numerous occasions in this book I have argued for a model of the media reader as an active, critical and often highly sceptical individual. My model of the media teacher has been based on this view of the media reader. Logically therefore, one part of my argument, especially in this chapter, has been to invite the teacher to put aside anxieties about and a distrust of media-related work and so discover its value, its importance and also its enjoyment.

However, I anticipate that for some readers there will be a residue of concern about the affective power and influence of the mass media. This concern falls much more within the humanist than the Marxist camp, it is not an anxiety directed mainly at the oppressive ideology present in the media or even about the hegemony of current, establishment ideas, it is much more to do with a concept of the active but also *reactive* individual. In this view the individual is not simply being moulded by dominant ideas but reacts to powerful and catalytic stimulus; readers of a media text can experience emotions and sensations so strong that they are changed by them. Of course this is one of the claims made positively for 'serious' literature and drama, that it changes people's lives. For many people the difference between literature and *Boys from the Blackstuff* is in fact contextual. One must choose to go the theatre, even to open a book, but the act of switching on the television brings a potentially powerful text immediately into the room whether it has been individually selected or not.

Inevitably then, there continues to be, and will always be, a real debate about the dangers of watching material that is, for example, violent or sexual: how much can any individual absorb without becoming affected, perhaps permanently corrupted, by such exposure? The term 'video nasties' has become part of common speech and epitomizes such deep-seated anxiety about the potentially disturbing impact of audio-visual texts. In a similar vein, critics of the media worry about whether young viewers will be able to maintain any human sensitivity when they constantly encounter on news and documentary programmes scenes of appalling violence and suffering. Will viewers be able to distinguish between such real 'scenes' and the apparent reality of much television and cinema fiction?

I do not plan to take up these arguments in great depth here, they are the subject of much conflicting research. However, the fact that I am a great advocate of media education does not mean that as a parent and teacher I have no anxieties about potentially dangerous media effects. What I should like to concentrate on in this section is the teacher's role as organizer and mediator of media material and the relationship of that role to that of the pupils, in the ongoing debate about media effects. It is certainly illogical for any teacher who is especially worried about children's susceptibility to ignore the media. As I have already argued, the discriminate and resist model is not one I can support. The teacher's responsibility, as I see it, is to enable pupils to analyse and reflect on the production and consumption of media texts, including their own responses as an individual and as part of a group. This matter is the subject of a very useful discussion in *Television and Schooling* (Lusted and Drummond 1985) which examines the deep moral suspicion about television held by numerous powerful members of the professions and the civil service.

If we take as a starting point a well known feature of the tabloid press the Page Three girl, it is easy to recognize that the presence of such material in the classroom has immediate implications for a teacher and a class (whether mixed or single sex). This example provides us with a chance to look at the interrelationship between the comparatively static context of the newspaper and the whole range of concerns felt about the media. Any class invited to bring in a range of tabloid papers will almost inevitably bring in one, possibly many, examples of Page Three. A teacher has a number of choices, and here are four possibilities:

1 The pages might be removed or the teacher may have already insisted that no such pages be brought in. This is a clear and simple form of censorship and may be entirely appropriate although I would see it ultimately as self-defeating.
2 The pages are there but the teacher indicates that they are not part of today's topic. Unless working in silence some pupils are likely to talk about the pages in question and there may well be some informal discussion as a result.
3 The pages are not only there but they are part of the teacher's agenda. This agenda may be as censorious as that in (1), pupils are to understand that such material is offensive and those who agree with this view will be rewarded with the teacher's approval.
4 The pages are there, they are part of a particular media text and they need explaining in terms of agencies, categories, technologies, language, audience and representation.

This latter approach inevitably invites some pupils to express stereotypical views and opinions about the representation of women that appear entirely 'natural' and 'right' to them given the culture they have acquired. Equally some pupils will be angry and exasperated at such views and will seek to demolish them. I see the teacher's role as essentially a dual one. First there is a vital element of control, and this control lies in the realm of language. The way pupils discuss such an issue and the nature of their language is very legitimately the teacher's concern. However, the second part of the dual role involves control of a quite different kind. The control here can be best seen as a form of constraint. The constraint should be self-imposed and should restrict the teacher's tendency to dominate at the level of ideas; pupils will never discuss the real issues of power and prejudice that underlie Page Three unless they can discuss their ideas openly. The deep structures of sexism and male power are close to the linguistic surface in tabloid papers and can be investigated and understood if they are given proper and serious space.

Another major point relates to pupil understanding. Why should any adult expect a teenager to have grasped the full significance of Page Three as an icon of modern society? Adolescent views may be very sophisticated in their way but they will still be crude in others and often subject to rapid shifts. The teacher's judgement remains crucial and decisive in selecting what kinds of knowledge and understanding may be developed through discussion of such material.

To sum up my argument so far, the teacher, in this dual role, is working under self-imposed constraint, also recognizing the limitations that are inevitably a part of pupils' developing understanding. If there is dialogue about something like Page Three then this can only happen *between* pupils *through* the teacher's linguistic control. The teacher cannot call on some mythical moral consensus to put pupils to rights. Instead there are important perspectives on such an issue, these include, for example, feminist, religious, political and the pragmatically economic. Teachers can help pupils to understand why such material generates so much debate and to make their own positions perfectly clear without forcing that position on the class.

In essence I see the teacher adopting this role when it comes to any media work related to material that is by its nature controversial. In simple terms, and to state the obvious, the teacher has control over the selection of material used in the classroom but not anywhere else. Pupils will bring, between them, knowledge of far more media texts than the teacher has or needs to have but the teacher should avoid falling back on vague generalizations like 'Of course you will all have seen *Nightmare on Elm Street*'. What pupils will all have are feelings and opinions about violent and/or sexually explicit material.

What seems most important to me is that media education is about developing an understanding of where texts come from and what they are intended to do. Young people might become passive victims of sensational images if they were led to believe that such material is all-powerful, offering some kind of secret initiation into the adult world. If a class views a part of a highly popular and explicitly violent film such as *Terminator II* in school, then, whatever the similarities, they will not have the same experience as they would when viewing it at home on video or in the cinema. The teacher, in bringing in key questions of understanding, is engaging more fully the reflective and critical faculties of each individual.

All societies that have some degree of freedom must constantly redefine the notion of acceptability by identifying lines that only some groups may cross. The use of film certification is a simple example and the pupils themselves can bring their knowledge very readily to bear on this form of control. The pupils are a part of that process of redefinition whether they have any actual power to influence it or not. It seems to me that the relatively formal and structured nature of the classroom is the right place to discuss Page Three and 'video nasties'. Pupils have their own views about all these matters and need an opportunity to discuss them. In my experience pupils have their own worries and concerns about controversial material even if they have a healthy disrespect for some reactionary adults who seem to them misinformed and absurdly censorious. There is no tidy and simplistic opposition between teachers posing as moral guardians and pupils demanding increasingly explicit material. Instead there is a continuum of views, often well represented within a class, which moves and shifts in reaction to existing material that helps to define and redefine those views.

It may be that repeated exposure to certain kinds of audio-visual text has a serious consequence for some individuals especially if they are already vulnerable – for whatever reason. School is not the place where pupils will encounter such exposure. If a class was to study the use of images of violence on television and film then a teacher would need to be very careful in how this was approached; similarly with the discussion of Page Three. The care involved should be chiefly applied in structuring the learning experience of the pupils so that they penetrate below the surface to an understanding of the production of such material.

7 Making it work

This chapter is devoted to describing extended examples of media work and to explaining practical and organizational matters. No doubt some ideas in this chapter might be called my own but certainly the great majority stem from that mysterious process of assimilation which all teachers experience. My conscious sources are my own teaching, colleagues, students, pupils, published materials and, inevitably, the media.

The final chapter (Chapter 8) will examine how the media and media education are changing and the way an English department might organize itself to provide a coherent experience for its pupils. I hope that this chapter will illuminate the final one and vice versa.

Introduction

Before setting out various schemes of work I should like to sum up the underlying principles of media education in relation to English teaching.

First, a teacher's approach to media education, like most English work, must be recursive. You cannot 'do' newspapers or soap opera any more than you can exhaust the text of *Macbeth* with Year 9. What you have to do is select areas and decide on how they may be covered.

Second, the key areas of knowledge and understanding, agencies, categories, technologies, languages, audiences and representations can be tackled in a whole variety of ways. At times it will be productive to emphasize or concentrate on one but on other occasions such a division will only be confusing.

All the suggestions for work are suitable for mixed-ability classes.

Finally I shall not describe work in Media Studies but only those approaches that might be a part of mainstream English courses.

Newspapers years 7–11

I discussed earlier (Chapter 5) how there might be some danger of newspapers being done to death by teachers in their enthusiasm to provide opportunities for pupils to work within the journalistic framework. There is only one way to make the most of such a commitment to newspapers, and that is through systematic planning and with a conscious attempt to increase understanding with each return to the topic. I am not suggesting here that every time a teacher gives pupils the chance to write a newspaper report that they must be introducing new knowledge but I am arguing that a department can ensure that during the course of each year such knowledge can be incremental. What follows is a description of a short unit of work (2–4 weeks) for each year group that concentrates on newspapers and tries to build on previous work and to recognize the increasing sophistication of the pupils themselves. There are numerous points in the unit where other media are inevitably and rightly brought in; the focus on newspapers is to ensure that pupils can develop coherent rather than random understanding.

Year 7

I suggest that this unit might be done early in the year, it helps the teacher to relate secondary work to the primary school and provides some useful information about each pupil's interests in reading and in the relationship of that interest to the home.

The main aim here is to identify what pupils know about newspapers, to raise their awareness of what newspapers are for and to allow them to experiment with simple aspects of newspaper form and style.

Pupils can be asked to bring in examples of newspapers normally found at home as a resource for themselves and others. I will not repeat this obvious point with subsequent units. However, a less obvious point is that this helpful contribution also brings both reader loyalties and prejudices into the classroom. Often it is best to identify the specific purpose of the work before asking for contributions and, if appropriate, to clarify the need for as broad a range of material as possible.

Newspapers are very familiar, they need to be made less so. Most Year 7 classes can very easily produce a long list of daily, Sunday and local papers. A list can be generated in two 5-minute sessions. Pupils can then subdivide the lists into large and small size papers although this takes longer; the terms broadsheet and tabloid may be introduced by the teacher. At this point it is useful to question the familiar, an approach I use is to ask groups to explain the names of the papers and to decide whether the name tells us anything about the content. There is plenty to discuss and groups can be asked to go on to generate some alternative names that they feel are more suitable to papers they know.

A next stage is to ask pupils in groups to define newspapers by what they contain, i.e. what is in a newspaper and is there such a thing as a typical one? This approach is a simple form of content analysis; copies of papers are needed for pupils to go through noting pages devoted to different news areas and to other material. I advise that pairs undertake this work on one tabloid and one broadsheet paper. Findings can then be discussed and analysed. The obvious point that newspapers contain far more than news is often a surprise to many pupils; this is a good example of where implicit knowledge needs to be made explicit to be fully understood. The teacher can also begin some simple work on categories of news and help pupils to appreciate that papers are not all comparable, they have different functions.

Even at this age, approximately 11, I find that pupils are perfectly able to undertake close analysis of important aspects of newspapers. A simple approach is to buy four papers of the day, two tabloid and two broadsheet, and to pin the front/back page spreads up in the classroom and to gather the class around to ask them to describe what they see (denotation). If pupils have already carried out such work at primary school so much the better. The teacher can prompt with comparative questions whenever this seems useful. Once pupils have established points about size – i.e. of headlines, pictures, type and so on – and have registered the stories being covered they can move on to the relationships between pictures and words and to the style of headings (connotation). What are the papers trying to put across about themselves? On a suitable day pupils might compare how a story or an image has been used by different papers.

By this point pupils have covered a number of key aspects of newspapers and can benefit from a chance to play with their knowledge. The following ideas can be tried in any order to help pupils explore newspaper form and language: writing headlines for several different papers for a fairy story or similar well-known material, writing out headlines from several papers and asking other pupils to guess where they came from, removing adjectives from headlines and asking pupils to fill them in, making up a story and asking pupils to create suitable headlines for differing papers. All these activities both draw on and deepen pupils' understanding of newspaper form and language.

If appropriate, pupils might conclude their work with a more extended piece such as designing and mocking up a front page or producing a front page on a wordprocessor or by using a dedicated program.

Year 8

If a teacher can draw on a previous year's work like the above then a start can be made at a reasonably sophisticated level. The papers were treated in Year 7 as objects, categorized and played with but not questioned in any fundamental way. If groups of pupils are asked to consider what would be lost if newspapers were banned, perhaps because of a repressive law or because the world is running out of paper etc., they might find it hard at first to think of much real loss at all. News and entertainment are very adequately supplied by radio and television. It is useful once more to put the children into a denotative framework; given the adequacy of news coverage elsewhere etc. who reads papers? What do readers draw from them? Where do they read papers? Are papers read by more than one person? How many papers are sold in a day and so on?

Pupils will be able to draw on their existing knowledge to answer many of these questions but the teacher can supply the statistics if relevant. The class can then investigate through families and friends what happens to newspapers in those contexts, where people read them and for how long at a time. Pupils are likely to recognize that the newspaper audience is the same as the television and radio audience but much more compartmentalized by class, interests, job and so on by the newspaper they read; they may then be able to consider agencies, i.e. who benefits from the existence of all these papers, who owns them and what do they hope to gain from ownership? Such discussions can be far-reaching and can avoid simplistic conclusions.

The question of ownership links with ideas of selection. If pupils have retained their awareness of the essential differences between papers they can begin thinking about how they are made both at the institutional and structural level and in relation to technology. A way into this is through more advanced content analysis. If pupils measure the column inches devoted to particular stories they can work out which stories are receiving most attention and can then be asked to speculate on why? What is newsworthy, who decides, how is news gathered and who controls it? These questions provide the teacher with opportunities to look at roles such as reporter, sub-editor and editor and so on, to give some historical background to the way papers used to be made and how computer technology has changed production and to look at the idea of a news story.

Following a news story can be a very effective way to conclude this work. The teacher can be personally prepared well in advance, perhaps selecting and following a story or different sorts of story for a week or two before the newspaper work begins. Following a story can involve looking at how it 'breaks', how other papers pick up and use the story, looking at its narrative peak and then its sudden or slow displacement by other stories. This kind of study gives pupils the chance to develop a fuller understanding of how news is constructed. If, for example, the class works in groups and each group selects a story to follow over a week or longer, some are likely to find that their story barely lasts that length of time while others may find theirs becoming unmanageable. Once the class looks together at the stories, especially if each group has made a display/chart, they can then analyse and reflect on the process of news construction and question its validity. Pupils can also begin to analyse which kinds of story appear in which types of paper.

If a class, or at least a part of it, has the right momentum they can conclude this work with the creation of a fictional story. The story can be constructed from the elements of 'good' news stories, discussed and agreed on by the pupils involved and then written up. With a whole class each group can be given a part of the story and each individual a particular newspaper; the result is a spectrum of versions of the basic narrative that makes an exciting display.

Year 9

Pupils should now be ready to try to understand some of the more powerful forces at work within the media and to bring their own increased sophistication with language to bear on the language of the media itself.

The aim of this unit is to build on previous study of story and form by deepening pupils' thinking about concepts such as reality and representation. Pupils need to engage with the media in a mode that allows them to explore and interrogate its structures and to question its versions of significance.

Drama work can provide an excellent approach at this particularly self-conscious age. As always, to find a starting point that undercuts certainties is an effective beginning. I often like to begin work at this stage by trying to help pupils question 'news' reality. One, dramatic, way to approach this is by staging 'an incident'. Perhaps someone (another teacher or older pupil in role) suddenly does something in front of a class (steals a bag or a wallet, throws a 'prop' out of a window, stages a confrontation). This device, whatever it may be, is then revealed as such and pupils have to reconstruct it. Such an approach can be done equally effectively in drama with pupils 'knowing' all the time that the incident is a fiction. The denotative framework operates first: as a reporter, what did you see, what actually happened, can we reconstruct what went on? Can we make a group form an image to act like a photograph? What would the line under the photograph say to anchor the image? Then, moving more into the connotative, interpretative frame: why did the incident happen, what does it mean? If you were writing this up for a particular newspaper what elaborations might you make to turn the story into 'news'?

This beginning can be developed into a more full-scale drama in which teacher and class construct a story that can become media raw material. There are many possible scenarios, a bank robbery, a hostage crisis, an accident, an overdose, a natural disaster and so on. The pupils need to build up the story, creating a narrative sequence, inventing characters and so on until they are ready to examine how such are examined and represented by the media. Initially pupils can be reporters, coming to the scene, taking notes, photos, 'filming' what is going on. There can be meetings back at the office or telephone calls to the editor where the teacher in role might begin to prompt the story, perhaps asking reporters to look for stereotypes. Who are the heroes and villains? Is there someone we can blame for what happened? Press conferences can be staged to accentuate the pressure on the characters. The characters may have all sorts of comments attributed to them which are untrue, what can they do about this?

Through the reality of the drama pupils can investigate the powerful pressures of the media both for its subjects and newsmakers. Back at the newspaper office all these events need to be converted into print, using appropriate language, incorporating quotes from the characters and so on. The teacher, either in role or in ordinary class style, can focus pupils' attention on the formulaic style of papers, looking at lengths of sentences, insisting on the kinds of adjectives to be used, demanding rewrites and revisions, operating strict deadlines.

Similar work can be achieved through information technology using dedicated programs that simulate a newsroom experience or through other kinds of print-based simulations where pupils have to sift through incoming material and then select and rewrite it to a strict deadline.

Years 10 and 11

If pupils have covered newspapers in the depth described above then they should enter Key Stage 4 capable of using newspapers in their own work with the right balance of confidence and caution; a teacher can be far more selective in Key Stage 4, especially given the possible pressure of two GCSEs to cover. However, I would still advocate some work dedicated to newspapers but I will describe several possibilities for Years 10 and 11 without the detail of Key Stage 3. The following sections contain ideas which often involve opportunities to explore newspapers.

Although denotation and connotation have been used in previous work pupils at this age seem especially receptive to image analysis. Most teachers, in my experience, tend to use material from areas like advertising where the construction of the image is at once more careful and, often, much more finished than in the rough and ready world of the newspaper photograph. The use of denotation and connotation to read advertising images is highly productive and helps pupils to analyse images with more skill and in a more interpretive way in the future. Newspaper images can be as valuable as those from advertising because they appear 'natural', therefore their deconstruction can be both more challenging and more disturbing. Pupils are likely to be familiar by now with the idea of cropping but they can bring a more developed understanding to the process. Through image analysis they can examine the actual function of photographs in newspapers, comparing images from differing styles of paper. They can study key areas of representation such as class, gender, race, age, nationality and so on and look at the interplay between image and text.

The study of the representation of two groups can be highly illuminating work, especially if the two groups offer elements of similarity and contrast, for example teenagers and old people, young and middle-aged women, establishment leaders and opposition leaders, the rich and the poor, students and young unemployed and so on. As with the idea of following a story in Year 8 a teacher can create material by following two groups over a period just before the work with the class begins and so offer a current example of media representation. An important aspect of such work is the chance it provides to indicate absence as well as presence. In the representation of a particular group certain elements will always be remarked upon but others will not. Pupils can become aware of the nature and construction of representation by charting how a group is defined by what it is described as having and by the absence of other features used as characteristics of other groups. This kind of work is highly demanding and requires pupils to read very widely in order to gather enough material and then to read very closely in order to analyse and use IT.

Newspapers provide an extraordinarily rich source of language worth studying for its own sake. The following ideas are all well suited to combining Knowledge About Language and media education. Newspapers are one of the best sources for examples of contemporary persuasive language in editorials, letters, reports of speeches, polemical articles and so on. Pupils can gather and analyse these in relation to both rhetorical uses of language and the particular topics on which the writers are engaged. They can then produce their own analyses of such writings or create imitative examples. Newspapers all have their own political or societal position and pupils can analyse these through careful study of a range of examples from different sources. To some extent papers strive to have their own 'style' and pupils can look at this through comparing journalistic pieces to other kinds of writing, both fiction and non-fiction. Pupils can also investigate notions of appropriateness, the way papers tend to make conservative comments about language use but also push at its conventional boundaries. These various approaches to language might be offered to a class who can then divide by interest groups or take on research roles to report back to the whole class at a later stage.

Conclusion

There are many other types of newspaper-related work and I have, for example, left local newspapers out of my suggested activities entirely. There is no shortage of possible approaches and for this reason as much as any other, departments need to plan and agree on some common elements in order to provide their pupils with a reasonably coherent experience.

Popular fiction

I discussed the importance of popular fiction in the English classroom in Chapter 6 and so here I intend simply to provide two examples of units of work, the first to fit in with GCSE English and the second most suited to GCSE English Literature; this latter unit can be especially helpful with wider reading.

Writing popular fiction

I argued at length in Chapter 6 about the need for English teachers to rethink their rationale for the writing of fiction by pupils. Presuming that a teacher decides to encourage such writing how can a unit of work be organized?

The structure of this unit is as follows, initial reading and analysis of some popular fiction, deliberate imitation and, finally, developing a distinctive response.

In order to have a clear sense of the pupils' present interests it is helpful to carry out a preparatory survey of their current reading and viewing. This survey can occupy a homework or 20 minutes or more of class time. Teachers can devise their own questions, appropriate to a particular group. The areas I would aim to cover would be pupils' present enjoyments in reading and viewing, how much time they spend on these activities, whether they are solitary or social and so on. Reading needs to be defined as inclusive of newspaper, comic and magazine reading. I would also ask them to suggest what they think is popular amongst their age group and what they feel we should read and view in English at school. The answers to these questions provide considerable information and certainly give a teacher something valid to go on when discussing current interests with a class.

The answers will also identify what counts as popular fiction for that group. A teacher can then select what aspect or type of reading seems important and both choose examples and invite others to contribute some for class consideration. As with newspapers, pupil loyalties and prejudices will be rife and I do not find it productive to place any pupils in the position of having to defend their pleasures in reading. A much better approach is to help the class or groups within the class work towards conscious and deliberate imitation of some writing. What pupils need to decide early on is what kind of fiction they want to write.

Having made a tentative decision they can then study examples either individually or in pairs or groups. If their attitude is relatively negative, for example, boys suggesting that romance is ridiculous and sentimental or girls arguing that action stories are absurd and vicious then they may be encouraged to 'take on' such writing and find out whether their hypothesis is true and then whether they can imitate such work or not.

Pupils can now move on to the imitative stage. They need a clear brief and guidelines like the following will help. Their finished work should not attempt originality or parody. It should be a serious attempt to write a story that is successful in terms of the form. The writer must identify a specific audience and, if possible, find someone prepared to represent that audience and to comment on the story. This approach requires hard work and real discipline of thought. Finally the writer should produce a commentary on the piece explaining what has gone into the making of this fiction. The final piece of work can be assessed on the basis of the commentary and the criteria given above.

If the work has gone well and pupils feel interested in further development then they can move on to the final stage which invites them to use their knowledge more fully. Here the writing task is also precisely defined. Pupils can opt for originality; this requires them to write a story of their own either within a specific genre or not but with a commentary explaining what they have tried to achieve. They can opt for opposition; this requires them to subvert a popular form through parody, changing gender roles, flouting reader expectations and so on.

At the end of this unit the class or groups of pupils can reflect on the relationship between the reading and writing of popular fiction. They can try to sum up what they have learned, can compare with each other whether their views have changed and speculate about their future habits as readers.

Understanding genre

Genre may sound rather an off-putting term to pupils and teachers alike but its study has great potential, especially in Key Stage 4. One reason is because popular genres spread through all types of text and can provide insights into language as well as form. Pupils have plenty of existent knowledge to draw on and can soon produce an impressive list of distinctive genres by noting down how their school and/or local library and book and video shops are organized. This work can be extended into considering newsagents and categorizing not only magazines but their likely fictional contents, bringing in the way programmes and films on television are described and categorized in the newspapers, *Radio* and *TV Times*. This introductory work makes explicit to pupils that all types of fiction are organized and categorized wherever you encounter them and that such organization is not only a feature of places like libraries and schools.

A useful next step is to ask pupils who this organization is for. If the teacher draws up a triangle with readers, sellers and producers then pupils can consider the relationships between these parties, noting how the organization of interest categories helps but also restricts each of them. The class can then focus more specifically on readers. Why do so many readers want to pick texts that may be very similar to many others that they have already read? How many readers in the class tend to select their texts like this? Usually it becomes clear that most readers read like this for most of the time whether choosing print or media texts. Equally many readers can recall periods of their lives when they read everything by a certain writer or in a particular series and so on. As long as the teacher keeps the emphasis on texts and not solely on books then almost certainly all the pupils will be able to join in this general look at readers' habits. At this point the teacher can decide whether to focus a whole class on a particular genre, to offer material for a number of different ones that groups or individuals can choose from or simply leave all pupils to decide where their interests lie. The whole exercise can be used as a lead into a wider reading unit.

I think that there is a great deal to be gained by a whole class spending some time on genre in more depth, using two forms for close analysis. There are many forms that can be selected but choosing two with some contrasting and some similar elements can be very illuminating; for example, Romance and Crime. A class can then work on drawing up the basic elements of a typical plot, sketching out the usual characters and, possibly, identifying the kinds of language found in the two genres. Once the formulas are agreed then groups can create lists of texts that they either know or suspect fit these patterns and look for the way texts also subvert and distort aspects of the genre. The class can then bring in as many examples as possible for close analysis and display, including media texts of all kinds. There are plenty of interesting discussion points raised by comparing and contrasting the way the two genres are packaged and sold. Some unusual perspectives can be introduced by trying to decide which authors are the equivalent of 'stars' in films; book covers and posters make excellent source material to analyse.

The work outlined above may have covered enough for pupils and teacher and certainly it provides scope for good course work such as writing imitative examples of each genre (see the previous unit described above), mixing up certain elements, altering gender expectations within the stories, writing about and explaining the way the genres seem to work, writing reviews of particular texts from one or both genres showing how far they conform to reader expectations and so on. Some pupils may want to extend their understandings by applying this way of working to other genres whether they are already familiar with them or not.

If pupils are going on to produce a unit of work for the wider reading component of GCSE then the methodology outlined above can provide an approach, a way of working, that they would otherwise almost certainly lack. If they want to write about what they presently enjoy reading then pupils often have no distance from the material and so turn in several rather feeble plot summaries and no more. In genre work plot summaries are important but the plots become more visible to pupils as structures. Even when producing summaries the pupils are in an interpretative framework.

Documentary

Throughout much of this book I have emphasized the value of working with popular aspects of the media rather than arguing for the precedence of forms that are perceived by teachers as more respectable and serious like news, documentary and current affairs programmes. However, I am not suggesting that there is no space for these forms in the English classroom and have outlined several possibilities for working with them already.

Documentary may at first sight seem too demanding a form to explore if teachers take as their models *Panorama* or *World in Action*. I would argue, however, that documentary fits happily within English if defined in suitably broad terms. The act of documenting should be a part of every pupil's entitlement and some understanding of the form should be developed during Key Stages 3 and 4. I would suggest that documenting involves two basic processes, processes that can be complementary but also conflicting: one is the attempt to record, to capture the world; and the other is the attempt to explain it, even to provide a thesis about the ways of the world. In this sense pupils' work is on a continuum with *Panorama* though it need never attempt to emulate such a programme. Documentary work can take many, and varied, forms and I will cover only two examples here, one for use in Key Stage 3, the other in Key Stage 4.

You're not at the big school now

A subject I have often covered with a number of classes is the transition from primary to secondary school; I need not discuss here the traumatic nature for most pupils of this transition. This change marks a very significant rite of passage, one that is both universal for all school children but also particular to each school and each individual. I have described some aspects of my work with classes on the subject of primary/secondary transfer in *Moving On: Continuity and Liaison in Action* (Findlay 1987). It seems to me that the topic is a strong subject for Year 7 pupils but also a challenging one; can they document their own experience for the potential benefit of others?

In undertaking work like this a teacher can make an initial choice based on available technology. A class might make a documentary using photographs and words, on audio-tape, video or perhaps combining sound and pictures for a tape–slide presentation. I would suggest that the teacher thinks through some of the following points before deciding. It may be valuable if the pupils are a part of the decision-making process because then they will be thinking about the different technologies they might use. However, some pupils, especially ones that have not previously used these technologies, may unthinkingly opt for making a video because it seems more exciting as a medium. If this feeling of excitement drives the choice then that would guarantee plenty of enthusiasm at the onset but, all too often, produce considerable disappointment in the end; it may be best to encourage them to try first an 'older' technology.

The making of the documentary has a number of purposes. Its simplest one is to provide primary pupils with an understanding of the transition they are to face and with a view of their new school. For the pupils who are making the documentary this invites a number of questions. What is this 'big school' really like? Is it really the place they heard so much about? Are the stories about what happens to you actually true? Do we want to make the Top Juniors suffer and worry as much as we did? What do primary children actually need to know about secondary school? Can we tell the truth? A second purpose is to help pupils answer these questions and so think through some aspects of power and knowledge. They have knowledge, how will they use it? A third purpose is the investigation and selection of information. A fourth purpose is organizational, how can this large and diverse class produce one, collective and collaborative final product?

A tape–slide sequence can be a very effective format for a number of reasons. The first reason is that the class can decide on some overall structure and then groups can work on taking their photos, selecting the best ones and writing and recording their section of the tape. So with one camera, one slide projector and one tape recorder it is possible to complete the whole exercise; more of the same equipment is obviously very useful. The second reason for choosing tape–slide is that it allows for editing to be negotiated between the various groups with the teacher also involved. Sequences of photographs (which will become slides) or the slides themselves can be displayed with notes suggesting the commentary; all pupils who wish to can then make suggestions.

Once the sequence is completed it can be tested out on another Year 7 class and then used with top primary classes from the feeder schools. Pupils can take the sequence to a school and present it or it can be shown when primary pupils are visiting the 'big' school. Eventually those primary children can review the sequence when they have been at the school for two terms and either re-use and revise the original or produce their own.

A video can be made of the same documentary and whilst it is just as effective it has limitations that need considering. Most schools have one or two video cameras, perhaps even one per department, some children have them at home. In other words it is quite possible to have the use of several cameras. The disadvantage is that pupils may shoot hours of tape which then has to be edited for many more hours. In my experience a video like this has to be planned with more care and more restrictions than an audiotape or a tape–slide sequence. I have used the same overall framework as for the tape–slide with the class agreeing a structure and then groups taking sections. I always insisted on detailed planning and storyboarding with a very tight shooting schedule. Pupils have to set up interviews, make arrangements to video classes and organize all such arrangements well in advance of using the camera itself. I also expected pupils to produce some accompanying materials for the video such as teachers' and pupils' notes, a small accompanying booklet or work and quiz sheets. If the group has access to a Desk Top Publishing program and a video digitizer then the booklet can use key images from the video. These materials are useful in themselves but also provide a focus during the inevitable waiting periods between opportunities to use the camera.

The finished product can be used for the same audiences as the tape–slide; my own video efforts were always less polished looking than the tape–slide sequences but seemed to interest its audiences just as much. It might seem that after all this work the pupils who made the video would be ready to evaluate and analyse it but I would suggest that pupils of this age need a break, perhaps of several months, before reviewing their material. At this later stage they can afford to be older, wiser and more usefully critical of their own work.

Making an issue of it

At Key Stage 4 pupils can develop their thinking about documentary and their practical skills by studying the idea of an 'issue'. The purpose of this scheme of work is to help pupils to read documentary with more attention, to identify its conventions and constraints and then to explore this knowledge through production and reflection. There are three stages that might be followed. First, arousing interest in issues and considering their importance, looking at documentary as a form. Second, selecting an issue and appropriate technology for its documentation and then making a brief documentary. Third, discussion, reflection and analysis of the productions and of the light they throw on professional documentary.

In the first stage there are a number of approaches that can be used. Pupils can be invited to jot down on their own a list of issues that are important to them, then, in groups, to list issues that are currently important in the media. They can then compare and discuss these lists. Alternatively, a teacher and a class can identify two or three key current issues and carry out a media search for a week or more looking for media coverage and, where possible, collecting it. The class can then study the material reflecting on the nature of the coverage and observable differences between the way different agencies and institutions cover the issues. Another approach might be to involve the class in an attempt to identify one key issue about which the whole class would be prepared to sign a letter to their local MP. Individuals could begin by choosing their key issue and then move into groups to thrash out one agreed topic and so on until the whole class reaches (or does not reach) agreement. This latter process can often highlight the artificial prominence of an issue when so many might be chosen, this can lead to discussion of how the media select certain subjects and ignore others.

Any of these approaches can lead on to considering the way in which the media take on issues and so to the concept of a documentary. What is the definition of a documentary? Why is it such a high-status, comparatively unpopular form? What are its rules and conventions? How does it attempt to contain and describe an issue? The teacher can then show examples of documentary. It is useful to have some excerpts of beginnings and endings so that pupils can study these and the way they set up expectations. Pupils might then view at least one complete programme in class and be given the chance to watch and review for the class another one in their own time. Through pooling all their insights pupils can reflect on the nature of contemporary documentary and the features upon which it relies, e.g. the aura of seriousness created by music, presenter style and camera techniques, the use of interviews and linking narrations, the effects of voice-over and many others. By this stage pupils have a great deal to offer and the unit might conclude here with pupils writing critiques of documentaries and documentary style.

However pupils can be offered the chance to take on one of their issues or to select another, perhaps more local in emphasis and to produce a documentary of their own. If the whole class works together then the teacher may need to orchestrate a very precise but varied range of tasks to stretch the whole group. With this age group a more manageable and often more productive approach is to help the class divide into groups of children with a common issue that they wish to tackle. One method is then to give each group a deadline within which they must define their issue and how they hope to deal with it: they must also opt for an available technology. Most schools would be able to provide audiotape, video and photography. There is no reason why groups should not include drama within their scope. Usually it is best for groups to define their audience as their peer group but they might prefer to aim their work at, for example, younger children, parents, teachers, senior citizens or other defined audiences. The process of making the documentary might then be broken down into: research and preparation (for example setting up interviews), storyboarding and drafting, making (and remaking) the documentary, viewing and reflection. The period of time must depend on local needs but 2 weeks is an absolute minimum. For English teachers worried about written outcomes there are many opportunities for written work such as diaries of the process with a final reflective and evaluative conclusion, an essay style piece to sum up the pupil's views about the issue, an essay on documentary as a form and many others.

In the last stage the groups present their work either to the class or other classes and perhaps to their chosen audience if it differs from the peer group. There is then ample opportunity for the teacher to direct discussion and analysis at a range of concerns including the documentary process, the practice of professional documentary makers, the institutions that control the production of such programmes and the groups' revised or confirmed views of this particular media category.

Campaigns

The idea of pupils designing and executing a campaign has become a common activity in many English departments. The emphasis tends to be on one of two approaches: the first involves pupils taking on the role of an advertising agency and so designing a campaign to market a product; the second usually allows pupils to select a topic that they feel strongly about and to orchestrate a campaign to influence public opinion. Both approaches are highly productive, can be used with a range of ages and allow teachers to introduce or develop all the key concepts of media education.

I would expect pupils to be simulating campaigns in this way in Key Stage 3 and possibly Key Stage 4 but an interesting unit of work for older pupils can involve a 'real' campaign. I place 'real' inside the inverted commas because one of the points of such work is to show up the construction and orchestration of all campaigns and to analyse what exactly it is that they attempt to influence. Pupils at the end of Key Stage 3 or in Key Stage 4 can more readily reflect on their work and analyse its effectiveness and its relationship to professional practices. The approach below is one of a number that might be tried but it contains elements that could be used by any teacher in such work.

If pupils have carried out campaign work before then a valuable starting point is to ask them to reflect on what they did and what they learned. Equally it is also productive for them to spend a preparatory half an hour preparing notes on their current awareness, e.g. of existing local and national campaigns, political, environmental, charity based and so on, making lists of pressure groups and agencies, considering different tactics and levels of social action taken by the various groups. If there happen to be any important local issues to discuss then this can further enhance their initial thinking. Most campaigns involve an attempt to change attitudes and opinions but there are some that promote the resistance of change or even overturning change. It is very useful for a class to consider what individual campaigns or agencies are attempting to do and to place them on two lines: one which has change at one end and no change at the other, the second which has no chance of success at one end and bound to succeed at the other. Pupils can add timescales to the latter line. A teacher can provide some insights into campaigns that have had an effect during his or her life or have become irrelevant over that time. While this preparatory work is underway pupils could also be collecting and looking at examples, discussing language and images, considering the various campaigns that are aimed principally at their own age group.

My own approach at this stage is to invite the class to experiment with change by selecting a campaign topic with real possibilities and by trying to decide how change might be demonstrated. It is very easy for a group of Year 10 pupils to identify, for example, many things that they would like to change about school or the way they are treated at home but it is difficult and even painful to find an agreement which satisfies the whole class about one feasible topic. I ask the class to agree on a topic or to decide that they cannot and, if the latter, to stop there. Other teachers might prefer to allow groups to choose and so avoid the painful process of finding a compromise agreement. Various approaches can be used to generate a topic; brainstorming on the board and then voting; groups working on a list of possibilities and presenting their case; individuals given a minute or two to put forward an issue of importance.

Once potential topics begin to come forward then key questions need to be raised as the process of selection goes on. What is it that needs changing – e.g. a rule, an attitude, something physical? Who controls the means to change? Who has influence with the controller/s? How will any change be measured? Could the attempt to change have an opposite effect? This last point is especially pertinent to teenagers who are the subjects of numerous campaigns about AIDS, smoking, drinking and so on. Are they aware of campaigns actually making any difference to their behaviour? Almost all these questions act as a potential brake on enthusiasm but they are useful in helping pupils to investigate thoroughly the actual process of change and the agencies that may constrain it.

After all this, an appropriate topic may emerge and three stages of work might then be identified:

1 *Finding out* – What do other people feel about our topic, do they want change? Do the controllers of the situation, e.g. the senior staff in a school, seem interested? What means have we got to effect this change, what will our campaign be like?
2 *Action* – Carrying out the campaign over an agreed period of time.
3 *Evaluation* – Has anything changed and, if so, how do we know?

The first stage can involve interviews with key people or 'the pupil in the corridor'; questionnaires and surveys can be undertaken; letters can be written with requests for information. All of this helps pupils to compare their own perceptions of what might change with those of others; it also provides excellent insights into the relationship between public 'opinion' and media representation. If stage one yields the right kind of information then the group can decide to go forward with the second stage. The teacher may wish to consult and discuss with colleagues about this next stage as it might have implications for them; certain pupil-chosen changes could be the subject of considerable opposition amongst other staff either because of the proposed change or because pupils are the agents or both. Pupils need a realistic awareness of these issues. The second stage requires the dissemination of the information gathered in a variety of ways using some materials from this list, posters, flyers, brochures, handouts, letters, speeches, special meetings and lobbying. Whatever happens the group can then attempt to measure whether there has been any change in attitudes regardless of whether the proposal succeeded or not. This stage may involve follow-up interviews, question-naires, etc.

The whole approach to a 'real campaign is far more fraught for teacher and pupils than a simulation. I hope that I have made its particular chal-lenges clear in my description. Although it should not be undertaken lightly it offers scope for insights into the whole concept of campaigns and public opinion in a powerful way. Whether the change happens or not, or if pupils decide to stop quite early in the process the overall effect is not lost. There is ample material for reflection whatever the outcome.

8 Media education, English and the future

In this final chapter I will attempt to look ahead and to offer some suggestions about possible ways forward for the combined forces of English and media education. As nothing has changed faster in the last 50 years than the media such an attempt must be a combination of judgement and intelligent guessing. But if the media are ever changing and the spectacular progress of media technologies continues, yet such a state of flux also produces some constants and some continuities. We already know that the media are subject to the same short-term views as are older communication forms like books. With books every change in the means of production or any shift in the borderlines of censorship cause outcries about the end of civilization as we know it. So with the newer forms – television, film and so on – there is a constant public anxiety about children becoming video zombies or adults turning into couch potatoes. If there is any fundamental truth in these concerns then we certainly lack supporting evidence at this late stage in the twentieth century to make such judgements. This is an example of a paradoxical consistency: the rapid changes in media technology produce a constant flow of very similar reactions of anxiety.

In the world of education the 1980s were a decade of extraordinary change, the implications of which are by no means clear. The rapid development of media education is in many ways representative of this traumatic period. Media education currently has an 'official' home in English, continues as a specialist subject at GCSE and has a place in A Level and in higher education, yet its position and its status are by no means secure. I anticipate, however, that in spite of this, slowly and unsystematically, media education will grow. In the course of this growth both English and Media Studies will change. In some schools media education across the curriculum will become an increasingly important curricular element but I very much doubt that there will be any 'official' support from the National Curriculum Council for this initiative unless there is a radical change in the political climate.

It would be all too easy to make this section a blur of statistics and numerical predictions and so I think it much more appropriate to concentrate on the *nature* of the changes and to consider possibilities and ideas.

Changes in the media

The pace of change in the media may be very fast but there is nothing to stop English teachers making the most of the latest technologies to enhance their teaching and pupils' learning. I have picked out what may be the most useful technical developments of the last few years, giving some idea of their scope for valuable work in English and media education.

Information technology and media technology

For the English teacher one of the richest areas of development is the increasingly dynamic interface of information technology and media technology. I have already discussed some types of software like desk top publishing and news simulations. The regular use of these kinds of software are well established in some schools and developing in most others. However there are still far too few machines (see the figures in POST 1991) for most pupils to become sophisticated users of such software. It is still the case that the great majority of student teachers start their education courses with little information technology experience and this is particularly true of English specialists (for details of this point see *Information Technology in English in Initial Teacher Training*, Goodwyn 1991b). Student English teachers who do have IT experience have either gained it through having worked in other, usually commercial fields or through having a machine of their own at home. However, within the next 2 or 3 years some students will be coming into teaching who have already worked extensively with IT as pupils. This change will not only improve the IT competence of future teachers but it will enhance their capacity to use IT to support learning in the media education field. There are several ways that this competence might best be used and I outline some possibilities below.

An area like electronic mail offers a fascinating cross-over between media work and IT. In some ways it is simply a particular means of delivering a written message. When a writer produces a letter in electronic form and sends it to a mailbox for one or more readers then the delivery of a message is perhaps all that is involved. However, if, for example, the writing is 'live', and various writers are communicating directly then something different is happening. The medium begins to affect the language; there is a mixture of conventional writing and a kind of chat. The writers may or may not know each other and so there is potentially both direct contact and yet more mystery than with many other forms of written communication. At first one might consider this simply an IT matter. There is usually only one writer writing at a time and the total participants amount to two. However, technically, there might be far more: large numbers might receive messages through e-mail and have the opportunity to respond instantly right across the world. This potential for e-mail to be more like mass communication or, at least, multiple communication, makes it a most exciting and, as yet, undeveloped resource.

A small but significant number of schools have been experimenting with e-mail links with other schools in other parts of Britain and, increasingly, in other countries. Now that messages can be stored and sent at relatively inexpensive times, e.g. in the middle of the night, cost is not a prohibiting factor. In effect, a class can communicate with another class across cultural boundaries. It might be the case that a group simply sends many individual messages to other individuals but very often the groups have to agree on and adopt a communal message. This form of communication then becomes close to that of others such as advertising and newspapers. There is an audience that is both known, e.g. perhaps identified as a group of high-school American students but still unknown because it is invisible. The communicators must make some assumptions about their audience in order to be understood but must also test out these assumptions in order to refine them. The attention to audience provides very interesting parallels with media audiences.

Finally, e-mail becomes exactly like a mass medium when one user is able to send a single message simultaneously to hundreds of receivers to pick up in their 'mail boxes'. Such potential raises many intriguing questions about a new form of service/electronic junk mail.

Fax machines

Many secondary schools now have a fax machine and all will have one eventually because they are both inexpensive and useful. They are as yet unexploited for learning purposes but that may soon change. The fact that a fax can send an exact copy of text and images allows for some interesting possibilities in media work. Pupils can send finished examples of their own work, drafts of materials they are working on, cuttings from magazines and papers, photographs, any number of items. The same facility is available using an envelope and the postal service but the important difference at present lies, as with e-mail, in the instantaneous nature of the communication. Classes from different parts of the country could be cooperating on a media project, the joint production of a magazine for teenagers for example, and they could exchange ideas not only about text but also about layout and images; messages and drafts could pass back and forth, with comments, within the space of a conventional lesson.

Satellites

The dramatic initial claims, made chiefly by media corporations, for the impact of satellite television on the nation's viewing habits are now scaling down to far more modest proportions. Most children still come to school knowing what satellite transmissions can do but with little or no direct viewing experience. My guess is that satellite television will become increasingly part of the normal domestic scene over the next 20 years.

Schools, however, have every reason to exploit this marvellous resource for educational purposes and no curriculum area could be better served than media education. Satellite can provide access to every category of media text produced by a different country and so can allow thorough and detailed comparisons with British texts. Pupils can study what counts as news in several countries on the same day. They can examine what soap operas are like in other countries and varying cultures. They can examine and attempt to explain what makes certain kinds of programme popular in all countries whereas some forms clearly have to be adapted.

Inevitably such material may generate a high level of cultural stereotyping in pupils but such responses are also material for analysis and reflection. I look forward to the day when a class in Britain might watch a French programme while a French class watches a British one and the two groups question each other via e-mail in order to understand the codings and meanings embedded in each text. The value for language learning at the same time is immense. I hope that English, Media Studies and Language teachers will recognize the potential for all of them that might be exploited by maximizing the way satellite broadcasting is used by pupils. It is not that pupils need to view many programmes but that they view them intensively both for their foreign language learning and media understanding.

Video

Video may now be as ordinary and everyday as television but one consistent element throughout this book has been the suggestion that this very ubiquitousness makes it an under-exploited resource. Its technology allows for teachers and pupils to investigate, analyse and play with a whole spectrum of texts and to question rather than merely accept their messages and meanings. We are still a remarkably long way from making full use of the power of video technology in its present form and there are numerous suggestions throughout the book about making far more effective use of taped programmes and the video camera.

One likely effect of the spread of portable and cheap video cameras is that many families will soon have video archives. These might seem at first to be only a version of the photo album. However, it is worth considering these tapes in two ways.

First, yes, they are like a photo album and at present we rarely make much educational use of these. Some children include photos in their autobiographical work or in writing about their families but this is barely to scratch the surface of the potential of such rich material. Many families now have automatic or polaroid cameras that make the need for technical expertise far less important than in the past. This change is important in freeing more people to be active picture takers although it may eventually lead to more mystification about the photographic/developing process as the technology requires less and less technical knowledge to operate it. Media educators in general can overcome such a problem by encouraging some technical understanding where appropriate. So, in a similar way, the domestic video camera allows everyone who can afford it to capture events, changes, whatever they like and to review and edit these for a number of audiences. The family photo album and the videotape contain vast amounts of meaning for a very small audience but they also contain considerable meaning of a different type for a much larger audience.

Once the potential embarrassment and inevitable possessiveness of pupils about personal photos and tapes are overcome – and this is a valuable area for discussion in itself – then such material offers great scope for looking at how people capture themselves. This becomes material that can be discussed as documentary in the true sense of recording exactly what happened but also where the presence of the camera actually affected not only the behaviour of the participants, i.e. it partly controlled the events or scene but it is still only a partial record that may be analysed as such with a 'witness' from the scene itself. Inevitably much of this material will seem potentially dull and uneventful to the majority of viewers. Such a reaction can then be used to compare and contrast with the flow of texts from the media, particularly television.

The second use of this archive material is for collective and collaborative work. The existence of the materials allows groups to select key scenes and images and to re-present them for a new audience. This work might be strictly autobiographical, perhaps a group of Year 10 pupils create a short text about being a child in the previous decade. However the same group could explore aspects of gender, how did boys and girls become what they are? What influences are apparent in the way the two sexes were being treated and shown to the camera? In this way the video archive becomes no longer solely a personal record but provides collective evidence for analysis and interpretation.

We also need to address ourselves to issues that arise from the nature of children's experience in an age of video. For example an interesting effect of children's potential to learn more because of their increasing recognition of how the media work can be revealed in areas like Drama. I find children (and adults) much more able to perceive the value of reviewing some drama work because they can conceptualize their text like a video; hence freeze framing, slow motion, editing and re-editing a narrative are more readily understood and enjoyed now than even a few years ago.

Still video

The still video camera might seem like a contradiction in terms but once its technology is explained its importance becomes very clear. It must be said that it is a new piece of equipment for schools but it looks a marvellous resource. It is very simple to use. The camera is palm size and takes full colour pictures in a similar way to an ordinary still camera. The images are recorded onto a two inch wipeable floppy disc that takes up to fifty pictures. The camera can then be plugged straight into a television using the aerial socket and the image shown immediately on the full size of the screen. The camera also has a 'macro' mode that allows small objects or illustrations to be made into images and then immediately shown on the television screen. The camera also has a time lapse device allowing for a delay of between 1 and 99 minutes. Images can be transferred to video using a simple lead and then sound track added. There are other features either developed – like the film converter that allows for negatives and slides to be copied on to the disc – or now under development, such as a PC kit which allows images to be transferred into a DTP environment and so provides ways of printing the images themselves.

The vital point about this camera is that it lets anyone capture images and then talk about them. The emphasis is on the interaction between the image taker and the active audience. An English teacher might take images of twenty current magazine advertisements and discuss them with the class and then ask groups to select five of their own to demonstrate to the class. Before making a video documentary or a narrative the pupils might use the camera to create extensive storyboards as a draft for their actual production. The possibilities seem endless.

Interactive video

This technology has so far made only a tiny impression on schools but now has the support of agencies like the National Council for Educational Technology and may be more influential in the relatively near future. It has the potential to be a very valuable resource in many curriculum areas but I have also seen some use related to media education and it seems best to illustrate its potential through example. A video disc can contain hundreds of snippets of still and moving images, sound and text pre-selected in some way. I have seen an American disc which has the Arab–Israeli conflict as its theme. A group of pupils could view the material and then 'mark' and select various sections to use in their own documentary about the conflict, presenting this to their class. As the resources grow so the potential for interaction should grow too.

CD-ROM

Compact Disc, Read Only Memory. CDs are becoming a standard format and more and more listeners are buying them for the quality of music reproduction. Even basic CD players allow a teacher to program a sequence of tracks which has interesting applications for pupils determining different approaches to a conventional 'long playing' record.

The really exciting area for media education at present is the power of CDs to store information. During 1990 and 1991 various newspapers – *The Times*, *The Independent* and *The Guardian* for example – began to offer large amounts of their copy on CD. This means that pupils could search almost a whole year's output from one or more papers using key words, key names, following a story and so on. The *Guardian* disc, for example, allows a user to scan all the front pages over a 6-month period, providing not just a sense of news content but also its presentation and accompanying images. However, the approach users are able to take is entirely dependent on the facilities built into the material. Therefore whilst pupils can only follow pre-set patterns they are now at least free to rifle through texts and to study and reflect on a whole range of issues about the manufacture and control of news.

As libraries, some homes and some classrooms, become better equipped so the potential to use this facility may increase dramatically. Equally if this trend continues and more and more of such material becomes available so pupils and teachers should have more control over how to use and analyse such banks of resources. Older pupils working towards a Media Studies qualification are likely to be the most immediate beneficiaries of this technology but I would expect pupils of all ages to find it valuable. Pupils in Key Stage 3, for example, might develop their persuasive writing by looking for information to back up a particular point of view.

Can there be more?

The above list is not comprehensive and becomes out of date as I write it. However there is no reason for English teachers to feel bemused, overwhelmed or irritated by concerns about being up to date. My intention is simply to show how changes in technology offer rewarding ways of helping pupils improve their understanding of the media. It is up to each department and then the individual teacher to decide what best use to make of these technological opportunities.

English and Media Studies

I have argued throughout the book that the majority of media education is best placed in English in Key Stages 1–3. I have also argued that as only a small number of pupils, 10,000 in 1989 (Blanchard 1989), choose, or have the opportunity to choose, GCSE Media Studies then English at Key Stage 4 must for many reasons continue to develop all pupils' media understanding.

There are a number of useful surveys of courses and syllabuses, all produced by the BFI (BFI 1989, Blanchard 1989), some in conjunction with The Scottish Film Council, and these will help any teacher to survey the field and to select which courses might be best for a particular school. As descriptions of current practice, however, all these surveys will be in danger of becoming redundant when the National Curriculum and GCSE collide. As I write the level of coursework in all subjects is being restricted and, in English, radically reduced. Media Studies seems certain to suffer a similar fate. The immediate question may well be whether Media Studies will survive in its present form no matter how popular it is, and might become, with pupils and teachers. Equally, if GCSE Media Studies emerges from the collision, what will happen to important elements such as practical work if coursework is radically reduced? There is so much uncertainty that speculation here seems of little value. Media Study as a critical and as a vocational course exists in many forms in higher education and seems to have a solid base there for the foreseeable future (Blanchard 1989).

I am led to the conclusion that English may be carrying even more responsibility for media education in the 1990s than before. For this reason, amongst others, the current dialogue and productive argument between English and Media Studies must continue. There is a very powerful and well-established argument for Media Studies at 14+ which needs no rehearsing here. However, even with the establishment of a new association for media education, launched at a conference on 1 November 1991 (see *The Times Educational Supplement*, 8 November 1991) there may be considerable difficulties ahead in maintaining the momentum of media education.

In order to consider the future of English and media education I should like to review ideas from earlier chapters and to conclude the book by bringing together a number of key concerns and attempting to sum them up. From this base I should like to sketch the place of media education in English for Key Stages 3 and 4, making some suggestions about the way English may evolve as a result of giving more systematic attention to media texts.

Media education in English, the way forward

Principles

If an English Department intends to review its current practice and introduce a more coherent and systematic approach to media education then it will need first to evaluate its existing media work, identifying which areas teachers already cover and what resources they use. This process can then help with identifying the needs of individual teachers and of the department for future development.

The following list of statements may provide a useful means of reviewing current practice. The question following each statement may act as a starting point for discussion:

- Pupils, regardless of age or ability, have a great deal of expertise about the media. (How can this expertise be best used and developed?)
- Pupils' media knowledge tends to be implicit and can be made far more explicit through active approaches to the media. (What kinds of activities make pupil's knowledge available to them in the classroom?)
- Pupils' interest in the media can be used to stimulate development in all four language modes (speaking, listening, reading, writing) and can address all National Curriculum Attainment Targets in English. (Where can media related work complement and extend existing good practice?)
- Reading the media is partly developed through the act of reading but close media reading is a learned and teachable skill. (How can pupils in each year group progressively improve their ability to analyse and reflect on media texts?)
- All texts, including the full range of media texts, are worth investigating. (Can teachers develop an approach that avoids simplistic value judgements and helps pupils to question their own?)
- Practical media work for pupils has the same relationship to professional production as reading published stories has to pupils writing their own stories. (What kinds of practical media work help children to understand about making meanings without producing invidious comparisons with professional standards?)
- Media education helps to make links between pupils' everyday experience and their work in English and in their education generally. (How can teachers help pupils to recognize the constructed nature of media meanings? How can the 'normal' and 'obvious' be problematized?)
- Media education can and should happen in any subject but English provides the basis from which other departments can develop their work. (What links can be established through media work with cross-curricular themes and dimensions and with other departments?)
- The development of an understanding of the media is similar to language development, it is neither linear nor hierarchical and is closest to a recursive model; rather like a spiral broadening out as it grows. (How can teachers ensure that work on the media continually brings pupils' developing understanding to bear on key areas whilst avoiding redundant repetition?)

Practice

It is important that a department has at least one teacher whose responsibility is to monitor media education in the department and the school.

However, it would be a great mistake to expect an individual to have all the ideas about media work. All teachers must contribute to media schemes of work and the trying out of new resources and approaches. The department needs to provide time for considering and discussing media education particularly in the early stages of developing new modules or schemes of work. There may be local advice available to provide in-service sessions. When it is ready, a department needs to look at a list of statements such as the one above, review existing practice and develop a plan for integrating media work, possibly over a period of years. There is no need for a departmental approach to limit the originality and interests of individual teachers. There should be scope in such a plan for every teacher to contribute their individual insights but within the agreed framework of the department's policy.

I outline below what might make a reasonably coherent approach to media education in English paying attention to National Curriculum demands in English and to cross-curricular themes and dimensions, pointing to possible links with other departments where appropriate. Two very practically minded books provide excellent material for integrating media education in English and have sections which complement the one below (Grahame 1991, Bowker 1991).

There are several points to bear in mind when planning the media education sections of the English curriculum:

- Pupils should, over 5 years, cover all the main elements of the media: television, film, video, radio, photography, popular music, printed materials, books, comics, magazines and the press, and computer software. The coverage of these areas will, on occasion, be spontaneous but the majority of such work needs careful planning to ensure that pupils build on previous knowledge and that work undertaken by other departments is not ignored or duplicated.
- Pupils should regularly be addressing these key questions and media areas:
  Who is communicating and why? (agencies)
  What type of text is it? (categories)
  How is it produced? (technologies)
  How do we know what it means? (languages)
  Who receives it and what sense do they make of it? (audiences)
  How does it present its subject? (representation)
- Pupils should have a developing awareness of the complex production of all texts and their own increasing sophistication as reader and producer of texts.
- Pupils should have clear opportunities to become more technically proficient through practical work; by the end of Year 11 all pupils should have worked with videotape, video camera, audiotape, tape recorder, a still camera and photographs, television, radio, film (in a cinema) and

Table 2   Example of a framework for Media Studies

Year	Term one	Term two	Term three
7	Newspapers and magazines	Children's television	Documentary
8	Words and images	Comics and magazines	Adaptations
9	Soap operas	Film of the book	Campaigns
10	Shakespeare	Newspapers/media simulations	Popular fiction
11	Documentary	Media and language	

computers. It would also be highly desirable for them to have encountered newer technologies such as the still video camera, e-mail, fax and CD-ROM.

Table 2 is just one example of a framework upon which a great deal might be built; I do not intend here to detail the lessons and activities that such an approach would require, particularly as almost all the topics have been covered in some depth in earlier chapters. Instead I will concentrate in the text on explaining what the framework should achieve, first by commenting on each year and then by reviewing the whole curriculum. I have placed the names of departments in parentheses where the topic offers opportunities for direct interdepartmental collaboration and the title of a cross-curricular theme in square brackets where it might usefully be incorporated into the topic itself.

Year 7 would cover a wide range of key media areas and identify and build on work from Key Stage 2. By starting with newspapers and magazines pupils would review and then extend their existing knowledge and being to work in analytical and practical ways on media texts. They would consider the varying value judgements made about the press and reflect on what their own might be [citizenship]. Later they would work on television made 'for them', considering the institutions of television and some of the economic forces at work [EIU] (Drama). By looking at documentary they would explore non-fictional aspects of the media and analyse the process of presenting cases and opinions [Citizenship] (History/Humanities). These three units would provide a firm basis in media education for all pupils, helping them to see such work as integrated within English.

The first unit in Year 8 might include a number of elements, looking at book covers, advertisements, photographs and posters, T-shirts and record/CD covers, pupils probing at the way words and images interact and create new meanings (Art/Technology, Music) [Environmental Education]. Pupils might then undertake an extensive survey and analysis of the readership of magazines and comics, considering the nature of such 'entertainment' and issues of gender and race representation, the pressure of peer groups and the media (Maths) [Health Education, EIU, Citizenship]. The class might then trace a narrative in its various media forms, considering the idea of adaptations, of media forms in general, categories and genres (Drama).

At the end of Key Stage 3 pupils might investigate the soap opera genre, looking closely at audiences and narrative devices, moving on to look at a key media industry like film through developing their knowledge of adaptations [EIU]. By undertaking a study of campaigns pupils should pull together all the key areas of media understanding and try out some extended practical work offering a whole range of possible cross-curricular and inter-departmental opportunities [Health Education, EIU, Citizenship, Environmental Education] (Art/Technology, History, Geography).

I would hope that any Year 10 class would draw on its extensive understanding of the media in a variety of ways and in the course of all its English work but I single out Shakespeare because of the emphasis work on such a topic places on pupils and teachers to review the representation of important national – and international – texts. If pupils can reflect on the way Shakespeare has been mediated for them as well as working on some of the drama itself then such an approach should combine literary and media concepts in a powerful way (History, Drama) [EIU, Citizenship]. Pupils should now have enough knowledge for sophisticated and in-depth work on newspapers perhaps involving a considerable range of technology and allowing for a high level of practical work. As pupils grapple with the demands of 'unpopular' fiction they can reflect on the nature of fiction itself, the way books are produced and consumed and the astonishing power and importance of narrative in their society [EIU].

In their final year pupils could return to a high-status media form like documentary and through a combination of analytical and practical work try to understand what such a form means [Citizenship]. The last unit of work would provide scope for a final consideration of the role of the media in everyone's life and for a review of the understandings that pupils feel they have achieved; all national Curriculum themes and the work of other departments might be drawn on here.

This framework is not comprehensive, not all departments are mentioned, what of Science and Modern Languages for example? There is still plenty of scope for developing this simple model. Also the model itself is not intended to replace existing activities such as making a short radio programme about favourite poems or writing about Macbeth's death in the *Birnam Wood Gazette*, English teachers are bound to draw on media-related work on all sorts of occasions.

The reason a department needs some kind of model is partly because of the National Curriculum, and my example provides several opportunities in each Attainment Target to cover requirements in relation to media work. It also provides ways of returning to key media areas and concepts, helping teachers to identify pupils' development; progress can thus be mapped on to levels.

Good practice has no inextricable link to the National Curriculum and the other reason a department needs a model is to improve its practice. Units of work that are agreed by a department may be taught with individual flair and emphasis but pupils should still gain a coherent, incremental understanding. Such units of work can be properly resourced by the department, extended and improved. They can offer a basis for developing teachers' expertise, improving their sense of the way children grasp media-related concepts. Using this approach units can be revised and, when appropriate, replaced as the department builds a sound knowledge of the potential and quality of each topic. Equally pupils and teachers can build up an increasing technical competence, becoming more confident and more adept with a range of technology. The model can identify when pupils' technical competence could be improved and teachers can plan to improve their own in time for a module that may be new to them. As the model develops it will inevitably be part of a larger one designed to cover the whole of National Curriculum English for Key Stages 3 and 4.

As media education becomes genuinely an integral part of the whole model so it will be possible to test strengths and weaknesses. For example to what extent does media education help to improve pupils' Knowledge About Language throughout the Key Stages? Where can work with KAL help to extend pupils' understandings of the power of language in the media? Questions like these and the principles outlined above help a department to undertake a rigorous check of its written curriculum and of its actual practice.

The future of English

Once media education is integrated within English will the subject have become an even broader church than before, incorporating yet one more diverse and possibly divisive influence? My view is that it will be a rather different church and, as a subject, more coherent and better structured.

The difference will come partly from a resolution of some of the old tensions. Many English teachers continue to feel torn between the cultural heritage and the cultural analysis models of English. Inevitably all individuals – pupils, students and teachers – are caught up in this tension and it is actually a part of the process of, amongst other things, understanding how the meanings of a text can shift and change. Some of the tension should disappear for English teachers once they recognize that it need no longer be the mission of the English Department to single handedly stem the tide of mass media mediocrity. Instead the department can help pupils to read widely amongst a whole range of media, literary and non-literary texts. Pupils and teachers will attempt to understand the nature of these texts, the forces that produce them and their relationship to a multitude of other texts. There must be endless discussions about the relative values of all these texts,

English teachers will guide, advise and make their views plain but all the time the dialogue can continue. One firm, distinctive basis for English should be that it is text-centred, it will be a demanding discipline, insisting on an intensive engagement with the full range of media, literary and non-literary texts.

Being text centred will in no way reduce the importance in English of speaking and listening. In fact, because pupils study the flow of language in the media they will have an even greater chance to understand the power of speech and the value of active, critical listening. Their practical media work will provide them with a range of opportunities to experiment with their own speaking on audio and videotape and to engage in listening to their peers as well as media texts.

English will draw more extensively on pupil's existing knowledge, not just their direct experience as in the Personal Growth model. Instead of outlawing pupil's often extensive media reading it will draw it in and expect pupils to reflect on and make sense of what they have absorbed.

Pupils will have the chance to make meanings through images as well as words. In order to undertake such practical work pupils must develop analytical and critical readings of existing media texts. They can be encouraged to articulate their enjoyment of texts and to increase their pleasure in them through analysis and reflection. Part of this process will involve experimenting with meanings of their own and then considering these meanings in relation to those that have been professionally produced.

Ultimately English will be different: stronger, because less divided, richer because more open to the whole range of texts. I am convinced that there should be no dilution of quality in the English classroom. The study of soap opera might be intended to prove to pupils that soap opera is not very like Shakespeare but this would be a pointless exercise as pupils already know this. The study of Shakespeare can help pupils enjoy some of the greatest drama ever written, it will not in itself help them to understand soap opera as a phenomenon. A citizen of the modern world whose education has been of a high quality should be able to understand and articulate the importance of both Shakespeare and soap opera; the best educated will also recognize relationships between popular narratives – enduring or ephemeral – and their audiences.

Recommended resources

One of the clearest indications of the increasing popularity of media work in English is the rapidly expanding media sections of educational publishers' catalogues. My list is just a selection from this burgeoning field and I have adopted three simple principles:

- The majority of items are tried and tested and are known to succeed in English classrooms.
- Relatively 'new' items offer material that can integrate media education in English and help meet National Curriculum requirements.
- Each item has potential for media education and English work.

The English and Media Centre (Sutherland Street, London SW1V 4LH)

This was formerly the ILEA English Centre, producer of *The English Magazine* and a host of resources for teachers. It is now an independent centre, continuing to produce high-quality materials and now renamed to include media education in its brief. It works closely with The National Association for the Teaching of English and all its materials are available from NATE (Birley School Annexe, Fox Lane, Frecheville, Sheffield S12 4WY).

- *Choosing the News* – Exercises involving laying out and editing material for a local paper.
- *The Market* – A single A4 image of a market that can be cropped and altered to produce differing narrative effects.
- *The Visit* – A photo sequence of a thriller/suspense narrative that can be used in a variety of ways.
- *Teacher's Protest* – Images of a teacher's demonstration that can be sequenced to show how news selection affects reader interpretation.
- *Comics and Magazines* – Excellent A4, illustrated booklet, ideal as the basis for a unit on this topic.
- *Front Page News* – Source material for considering issues such as ownership, institutions and agencies.

- *Changing Stories* and *Making Stories* – Two complementary A4 booklets, not strictly media material but full of fascinating insights into narrative and intertextuality; can lead easily into considering related media texts.

The British Film Institute (Education Department, 21 Stephen Street, London W1P 1PL)

The BFI is now producing materials that are very suitable for work in schools and there are plans to provide a considerable range of new resources to help with teaching about the media in the National Curriculum.

- *Picture Stories* – Image analysis activities using sheets of stills and some slides with accompanying teacher's booklet.
- *Reading Pictures* – Three basic exercises in image analysis.
- *Selling Pictures* – Resources for analysing representation, especially of gender. The accompanying booklet 'The Companies You Keep' is full of dense, informative, case study material mainly concerned with ownership.
- *Criminal Records: Teaching TV Crime Series* – Photocopiable exercises and resource materials for genre study. Excerpts from actual programmes are available for hire from the BFI.
- *Hammer Horror* – Useful material on Hammer style horror and the genre itself.
- *Wham! Wrapping: Teaching the Music Industry* – A Case study of the group with masses of supporting material.
- *Media in English* – A new series which will provide materials for each year in KS3. The planned units are Children's TV (Year 7), Comics and Magazines (Year 8) and Soap Opera (Year 9).
- *Starters: Teaching Television Title Sequences* – Slides with accompanying notes on seven news and drama programmes.
- *Teaching TV Sitcom* – Slides and accompanying materials which cover a history of the genre and provide ways of analysing sitcom episodes.

Film Education (37–39 Oxford Street, London W1V 1RE)

A centre sponsored by the film industry that regularly produces free materials to support teachers working on a range of film-related activities. Schools should receive these materials automatically.

Publishers

Cambridge University Press

Making Meaning, Judith Baxter – English GCSE course book that contains several useful media-related sections.

The Newspaper File, Duncan Grey and Alysoun Hayhoe – ring-binder style set of resources intended to provide a full introduction to newspapers.

Teaching Television: 'The Real World', Andrew Hart – a kit for close study of how television programmes are made, includes resource pack, paperback book and videocassette.

S.W.A.L.K., ed. Linda Buckle – the film script of the serial of the same name; a video of the series is also available.

Gregory's Girl – The Filmscript, ed. Paul Kelley – the script of the film edited for classroom use.

Eye Openers (One and Two), Andrew Bethell – still one of the most useful resources for introducing a wide range of media concepts, there is an accompanying photo pack that can be copied, making practical work very easy.

Tales Out of School, ed. Paul Kelley – David Leland's four plays *Made In Britain, Rhino, Birth of a Nation* and *Flying into the Wind* edited for classroom use. A video of the plays is also available.

Collins

English in Action, Andrew Goodwyn (produced originally by Unwin Hyman) – an A4 book of photocopiable resources with accompanying teacher's notes. There are two sections aimed at each Year from 7–11, covering a wide range of topics. The book is specifically intended to bridge the present English/media education gap.

Heinemann

Read On, Susan Davis – a course style book for lower secondary providing genre based approaches to reading, includes several sections on media areas like advertising and newspapers.

Hodder and Stoughton

The following four titles were produced by the Scottish Film Council.

Local Heroes – A videocassette plus booklet that explores the story of a local Glasgow rock band examining in particular issues such as audience, industry and marketing.

Picturing Women – A book of photographic representations of women with commentaries by the four female photographers.

Open to Question – A videocassette and booklet examine the making of the BBC programme of the same name and of one episode in particular devoted to the views of Mary Whitehouse.

Bookmaking – A booklet which examines the book industry through a case study of Naomi Michinson's *Arcadia*.

Introducing Media Studies – a series of short booklets (48pp) designed to provide a reasonably comprehensive introduction to a key media topic. Titles include: *The Music Market, Making a Start, Reporting the World, Entertainment on TV, Looking at Films, Popular Magazines, Advertising in Action, Looking into Advertising, Newspapers, On Your Radio, Planning the Schedules* and *Thinking in Images*.

Longman

Writing for Magazines and Newspapers, John Griffin and Theresa Sullivan – a booklet which helps pupils to understand how the press produces a flow of a varying types of writing.

Making Adverts, Chris Davies and Hazel Hagger – a booklet introducing pupils to advertising and its techniques.

For and Against, Simon Fuller and David Meaden – a book to accompany the BBC English Time series of the same name. The book and the series focus on a series of issues, one of which is 'Watching Television'.

The Longman's 'Imprint Series' includes a range of interesting scripts, including two volumes of *Grange Hill* scripts and collections of TV and radio plays.

Nelson

Outlooks, Phil May – a 'student resource book' accompanied by a 'self-study book' which covers a very wide range of units for GCSE English. It includes sections on film, genre, television, radio, newspapers and soap opera.

Initiatives – A glossy series which includes a wide range of resources. Each 'cluster' includes a resource book, a repromaster and two audiocassettes. Clusters include *On and Off the Record* which focuses on reporting, documentary and news. The series also includes five topic books, four of which have interesting material, *Opening Up the Airways*, *Agony Column*, *Campaigns* and *Comedy and Humour*.

Oxford University Press

Media Choices, Jean Mills, Richard Mills and Les Stringer – a coursebook style introduction to media-related work in English covering a useful range of key concepts.

The Telebook, Chris Kelly – a behind the scenes look at how television programmes are made.

Bibliography

Alvarado, M. and Thompson, J. (eds) (1990) *The Media Reader*. London, British Film Institute.

Alvarado, M., Gutch, R. and Wollen, T. (1987) *Learning the Media*. Basingstoke, Macmillan.

Applebee, A. (1978) *The Child's Concept of Story*. Chicago, University of Chicago Press.

Association of Assistant Masters in Secondary Schools (1952) *The Teaching of English*. Cambridge, Cambridge University Press.

Barnes, D., Britton, J. and Torbe, M. (1986) *Language, The Learner and The School*. Harmondsworth, Penguin Books, 3rd edn.

Barthes, R. (1974) *S/Z*, trans. R. Miller. New York, Hill and Wang.

Batsleer, J., Davies, T., O'Rourke, R. and Weedon, C. (1985) *Rewriting English*. London, Methuen.

Bazalgette, C. (ed.) (1989) *Primary Media Education: A Curriculum Statement*. London, The British Film Institute/Department of Education and Science.

Bethell, A. (1981) *Eye Openers (One and Two)*. Cambridge, Cambridge University Press.

—— (1984) Media Studies. In J. Miller (ed.) *Eccentric Propositions*. London, Routledge and Kegan Paul.

Beynon, J. (1983) The politics of discrimination: Media Studies in English Teaching, *English in Education*, 17(3): 3–14, Sheffield, The National Association for the Teaching of English.

Blanchard, T. (1989) *Media Studies at 16+*. London, British Film Institute.

Bowker, J. (ed.) (1991) *Secondary Media Education: A Curriculum Statement*. London, The British Film Institute.

British Film Institute (1989) *Media Education in Britain: An Outline*. London, British Film Institute.

Britton, J. (1970) *Language and Learning*. Harmondsworth, Penguin Books.

Brooker, P. and Humm, P. (eds) (1989) *Dialogue and Difference*. London, Routledge.

Buckingham, D. (1987a) *Unit 27: Media Education* (EH207 Communication and Education). Milton Keynes, Open University Educational Enterprises.

—— (1987b) *Public Secrets: 'EastEnders' and its Audience*. London, British Film Institute.

—— (1990a) *The English Magazine*, (23).

—— (ed.) (1990b) *Watching Media Learning*. London, Falmer Press.

—— (1991) *The English Magazine*, (24).

Carter, R. (ed.) (1991) *Knowledge About Language and the Curriculum: The LINC Reader*. London, Hodder and Stoughton.

Clarke, M. (1987) *Teaching Popular Television*. London, Heinemann/The British Film Institute.

Collins, R., Curran, J., Garnham, N., Scannell, P., Schlesinger, P. and Sparks, C. (eds) (1986) *Media, Culture and Society*. London, Sage.

Cook, J. (1988) *Adult Education Film Courses*. London, British Film Institute.

Corcoran, W. and Evans, E. (eds) (1987) *Readers, Texts, Teachers*. Milton Keynes, Open University Press.

Davis, M. (1989) *Television is Good for Your Kids*. London, Hilary Shipman.

DES (1959) *The Crowther Report*. London, HMSO.

—— (1975) *A Language for Life*. London, HMSO (The Bullock Report).

—— (1984) *English 5–16*. London, HMSO.

—— (1986) *English 5–16: The Responses to Curriculum Matters 1*. London, HMSO.

—— (1988) *Report of the Committee of Enquiry into the Teaching of the English Language*. London, HMSO (The Kingman Report).

—— (1989) *English for Ages 5 to 16*. London, DES (The Cox Report).

Dixon, J. (1975) *Growth Through English*. Huddersfield, Oxford University Press for The National Association of the Teachers of English.

Doyle, B. (1989) *English and Englishness*. London, Routledge.

Eagleton, T. (1983) *Literary Theory: An Introduction*. Oxford, Blackwell.

—— (1985) The subject of literature, *The English Magazine*, (15).

Exton, R. (1983) The poststructuralist always reads twice, *The English Magazine*, (10).

Findlay, F. (1987) *Moving On; Continuity and Liaison in Action*. Sheffield, The National Association for the Teaching of English.

Glasgow University Media Group (1976) *Bad News*. London, Routledge and Kegan Paul.

—— (1976) *More Bad News*. London, Routledge and Kegan Paul.

Goodson, I. and Medway, P. (eds) (1990) *Bringing English to Order*. London, The Falmer Press.

Goodwyn, A. (1990) *English in Action*. London, Unwin Hyman.

—— (1991a) *The English and Media Magazine*, (25).

—— (1991b) *Information Technology in English in Initial Teacher Training*. Coventry, The National Council for Educational Technology.

Grahame, J. (1991) *The English Curriculum: Media 1 Years 7–9*. London, The English and Media Centre.

Greenwell, B. (1987) *Alternatives at English 'A' Level*. Sheffield, The National Association for the Teaching of English.

Griffith, P. (1987) *Literary Theory and English Teaching*. Milton Keynes, Open University Press.

Gurevitch, M., Bennett, T., Curran, J. and Woolacott, J. (eds) (1982) *Culture, Society and the Media*. London, Methuen.

Hayhoe, M. and Parker, S. (eds) (1990) *Reading and Response*. Milton Keynes, Open University Press.

Hoggart, P. (1984) Comics and magazines for schoolchildren. In J. Miller (ed.) *Eccentric Propositions*. London, Routledge and Kegan Paul.

Hoggart, R. (1957) *The Uses of Literacy*. London, Chatto and Windus.

Holbrook, D. (1961) *English for Maturity*. Cambridge, Cambridge University Press.

Inglis, F. (1969) *The Englishness of English Teaching*. London, Longman.

—— (1990) *Media Theory, An Introduction*. Oxford, Blackwell.

Knight, R. (ed.) (1972) *Film in English Teaching*. London, Hutchinson/British Film Institute.

Leavis, F. and Thompson, D. (1933) *Culture and Environment*. London, Chatto and Windus.

Lusted, D. (ed.) (1991) *The Media Studies Book*. London, Routledge.

Lusted, D. and Drummond, P. (eds) (1985) *Television and Schooling*. London, The British Film Institute.

Marcuse, H. (1972) *One-Dimensional Man*. London, Abacus.

Marland, M. (1977) *Language Across the Curriculum*. London, Heinemann.

Masterman, L. (1980) *Teaching About Television*. London, Macmillan.

—— (1985) *Teaching the Media*. London, Routledge.

Mathieson, M. (1975) *The Preachers of Culture: A Study of English and its Teachers*. London, Allen and Unwin.

Morsy, Z. (1984) *Media Education*. Paris, UNESCO.

Moss, G. (1989) *Un/Popular Fictions*. London, Virago.

Murdock, G. and Phelps, G. (1973) *Mass Media and the Secondary School*. London, Macmillan Education, Schools Council Research Study.

NATE Computer Working Party (1988) *IT's English: Accessing English with Computers*. Sheffield, National Association for the Teaching of English.

Packard, V. (1957) *The Hidden Persuaders*. London, Longman.

Parliamentary Office of Science and Technology (POST) (1991) *Technologies for Teaching: The Use of Technologies for Teaching and Learning in Primary and Secondary Schools, Vol. 1 Report*. Parliamentary Office of Science and Technology.

Potter, F. (1990) *Reading Learning and Media Education*. Oxford, Blackwell.

Protherough, R. (1983) *Developing Response to Fiction*. Milton Keynes, Open University Press.

Richards, I.A. (1929) *Practical Criticism*. London, Kogan Page.

Scholes, R. (1985) *Textual Power: Literary Theory and the Teaching of English*. New Haven, Yale University Press.

Thompson, D. (ed.) (1964) *Discrimination and Popular Culture*. Harmondsworth, Penguin.

—— (1969) *Directions in the Teaching of English*. Cambridge, Cambridge University Press.

Widdowson, P. (ed.) (1982) *Re-Reading English*. London, Methuen.

Index